COUNTRYMAN'S YEAR

Countryman's Year

by HAYDN S. PEARSON

Introduction by Dorothy Canfield Fisher

WHITTLESEY HOUSE

McGraw-Hill Book Company, Inc. New York London Toronto

COUNTRYMAN'S YEAR

PUBLISHED BY WHITTLESEY HOUSE

A DIVISION OF THE McGRAW-HILL BOOK COMPANY, INC.

Printed in the United States of America

To the Memory of

MOTHER AND FATHER

THE author is grateful to the editors of the following papers for permission to reprint essays: *The Boston Herald, The Providence Journal, The New York Times, The Richmond Times-Dispatch,* and *The Washington Evening Star.*

CONTENTS

FOREWORD

What, after all, in Haydn Pearson's writing do modern readers find? What is it, in his unpretentious pages which they like and keep on liking, year after year? To any casual observer, standing perhaps in a library or a bookshop and riffling over the pages of his books, they seem disorganized grab bags of heterogeneous odds and ends— comments on corn bread and blue jays and rural railroads and rocking chairs and splitting wood. There is, of course, a not-to-be-denied slight charm in pawing over the variegated contents of a grab bag. But everybody soon tires of mere scraps and tags.

Unless you are willing to look more closely and consecutively at a Haydn Pearson book, you will not see the qualities which have gradually drawn and held a large group of devoted readers. But not too closely and consecutively! Don't start on the first page and try to read straight through to the last, any more than you would start on Monday morning to eat consecutively all the meals and drink all the drinks of the week before you. Keep the book within easy reach, rather, in a room where you live a good deal, in your bedroom, or the kitchen (if you are a woman), or the family living room, and take a look at it, occasionally, wherever the volume happens to fall open in your hand. After a while you will have absorbed the reasons why a good number of American readers like to have Haydn Pearson around.

You will have seen that there is a unity in these apparently haphazard, discursive short pieces—they are all, you perceive after a while, written from a single point of view, a sure way to achieve harmony in any composition. The point of view is that of a country boy (not man, not woman, not girl) old enough to be considerably on his own in farm life, not old enough for any of the strained tensions, fevers, anguishes, and glories of adolescence. He is not so remarkable a boy as to be startling or formidable or at all unfamiliar. But he is fully human, with moments when he perceives and loves beauty—as well as when he revels in a growing boy's wild ravenous joy in eating.

Very infectious and engaging is this delight in eating. To be highly recommended to weary, bothered adults of small appetite, his placing on the table before us such fare as hot biscuits and new maple syrup, rhubarb pie (personally I don't like rhubarb pie, but Pearson casts a spell about it), corn bread, Indian pudding. The glorification in these pages of naturally-come-by, old-American fats and oils has something symbolic about it, I am sure, something which casts a light perhaps on what twentieth-century readers get out of the Pearson pieces. For his reiterated joy in rich yellow cream, poured over—well, over everything—and in fresh, farm-churned butter, is entirely in accord with the dicta of modern dietetic experts as to the basic importance of fats and oils in the human diet. He is speaking out of his own experience, his own vivid natural likings, and he is in accord with what scientific research has proved about human health. Reflecting on this point, one surmises that others of Pearson's interests and enthusiasms may spring from sound instincts just as deep, may remind us of (and help provide for us) some of the life-elements without which we would pine and dwindle, in spite of our twentieth-century appearance of abundance.

Remembrance of things past, for example. He is never pathetic, rather reticently matter-of-fact, about now vanished old-time doings like hunting eggs, digging potatoes by hand, going for the cows, picking apples for the winter use of the home, turning the grind-stone. He wastes no resentment, hardly any regret, on the shift in the organization of life which has rendered extinct hammocks under the trees, harness shops, tin peddlers, parlor organs, kerosene lamps, Saturday night bathing in tin wash tubs in the kitchen, root cellars, bag mending. He just reminds us in vivid detail that the present is not all, that the past did exist, and hence by implication that what now seems so overpoweringly all, may also become the past. Without harrowing your feelings, (this he never does, for any reason) he thus gently lengthens the everyday perspective in which you view life, and in so doing, refreshes your sense of proportion, which is always getting blurred by the modern demand to focus intently on what is, at any given moment, before the eye. "The world in general," he remarks somewhere in these pages, "is in a fretting irritable mood." Put the Pearson to your lips occasionally and take a little swig of something calming.

He is at the age, the country boy through whose eyes we see life in this volume, when his passion is more aroused by the lyric joy of a crusty slice of homemade bread fresh from the oven, richly spread with new butter and molasses, than by spiritual or aesthetic matters. But he is no barbarian. He has some poetry in him at times. And what is here has the lofty, supreme literary value of complete sincerity.

Note, to begin with, that he is no killer, although he is so wholly natural, so "plain" (in the rural phrase, meaning unpretentious), psychologically so unfettered, so impulsively free to be and feel just what he really is and feels. In all this kaleidoscope of country life, with its birds, its insects, its animals, there is not one moment of the hunter's joy in extinguishing life. When this boy goes for a walk, he carries no gun. The birds which fly, soar, sing, and flutter across these pages, are watched with an amiable fellow-feeling (with no scientific, cataloguing accuracy of wing-bars and counted tail-feathers, let me reassure you), but they are never targets.

Beyond this, although most of the book is unobtrusive, substantial prose, from between its plain words occasionally floats a lovely wisp of calm poetry—from, for instance, "Night Visit to the Barn."

Above all, this book is quieting. The author says in the "Barn Doorways" essay that "some countrymen have learned that resting comfortably is one of the most important arts of living." And, in a pleasant comment on winter, "Winter is the time of patience." And again, in passing, "Tolerance is needed in most phases of human activity." You will find here rest, patience, tolerance. You will not find stimulation in this book of life as seen in loving memory by a country boy. But most of us do not, not now, need to be stimulated. You may pick it up, with taut muscles and twanging nerves. You lay it down, calmer, more relaxed, with a fresher eye for what there is in life, everywhere, to enjoy if we can but look out on it with a seeing eye.

DOROTHY CANFIELD FISHER

THE MAGIC OF APRIL

STAND on a hillside in April and you can feel spring coming to an awakening land. You can feel it in the breeze from the southland. You can feel it in the mellow warmth of the sun's rays. You can see it in the inverted blue meadow that rests over the countryside—a blue meadow where flocks of shaggy cumulus clouds graze peacefully along the sky trails. You can see it in the swelling buds of the red maples in the swamps and in the fluffy gray kittens of pussy willows along the creeks and in the sloughs. You can hear it in the heart-lifting carols of the bluebirds in old orchards behind weathered barns and in the poignant, high-pitched calls of the wood pewees.

When the fourth month arrives, countrymen know that the stirring miracle of life's resurrection is on the way. Through the months of cold and ice Earth has taken her rest. Now the new season has come. In kitchen windows boxes of plants are lifting green leaves. By farmhouse doors lilac buds are bursting the stitching that has held the scales tight. Each day the sun takes a higher course across the heavens, climbing toward the pole of the horizons.

Snow shrinks in the windrows along fences and walls. Trickling waters course down pasture slopes and brooks sing a rollicking aria as the waters run high between their banks. Over the countryside there's the spirit of April. Men's souls stir to the surging tide, and hearts lift to the goodness of Him who ordains the cycling seasons. April is a month of magic, and man and earth respond to the goodness of the Great Spirit.

ULTRAMODERN sophisticates look down their noses at anything remotely tinged with Victorianism. In their judgment family albums are definitely a part of the spirit of yesteryear. Perhaps we are still too young as a people to appreciate properly the soul-satisfying traditions of previous generations, but time is catching up on this regrettable attitude.

The collection properly begins with a group of old daguerreotypes and ferrotypes. Great-grandfathers posed stiffly in their hirsute glory. In the nineteenth century beards and mustaches framed faces of solid, resolute character. Great-grandmothers used billows of petticoats and fetching bustles and seemed to favor high neckpieces of lacy, starched material. They piled their hair high and occasionally they went in for braids worn as a crown. But in the faces of those men and women, family likenesses can be seen.

At the turn of the century, styles were more daring. Beards were disappearing and the bustle was gone; petticoats were reduced to one or two. There were Gargantuan hats piled high with flowers and ornamental fruits. The girls, now grandmothers, had prim shirtwaists, ankle-length skirts, and high shoes. The boys specialized in tight-fitting suits and wide white collars. Through the years the procession continued. The changes in dress reflected the growing freedom of human beings as they emerged into the age of mechanical marvels. The bulky, billowy bathing suits gradually came nearer the irreducible minimum. The cars changed from horseless carriages to modern streamlined automobiles.

The family album is a part of our growing tradition; it tells the story of myriad changes. On a rainy afternoon when the children gather round the living-room table to see the pictures and hear the familiar, loved stories, they are learning a nation's history.

HORSE TRADING

AS it should be in a democracy, opinions vary as to what this country needs most. But high on the priority list the countryman would put the gentle art of trading horses. Time was, before the world was introduced to robot bombs, booby traps, and jet planes, when a man could court sufficient danger by letting it be known around the countryside that he might be interested in a horse deal.

Direct and decisive city businessmen would not understand the leisurely traditional ritual that is an integral part of a swap. When two horse traders meet, professionals or amateurs, the amenities have to be observed. By unwritten law such topics as the weather, crops, local, state, and national politics are discussed or cussed. Then by slow and circuitous paths the subject of horses is brought up.

The farmer is never especially interested in trading. Not according to his say-so. He has thought of it, yes. But not seriously. It is just one of those things. Old Jerry is a good, solid chunk of horseflesh. Maybe he pulls a little harder against the bit than he should. Yes, he is getting along. Let's see, he might be twelve, even thirteen years old. Just a trifle lame in the off rear foot. Nothing serious. A few weeks in pasture would clear everything up. Old Tom? Nothing wrong

3

with him. May kick occasionally when startled, and chews the wood in his crib. But a good, strong horse. Lot of work left in him. Age? Possibly thirteen, or might be fourteen. Hard to tell in a big, rugged horse like him.

We countrymen do not pretend to be authorities on international diplomacy. We never ran an allied conference with a score or more nations taking part. Could be, however, that if the government saw fit to include a few really first-class horse traders in our delegation, the average citizen would be less apprehensive about the results.

SPRING RAIN

THE dictionary is terse and prosaic concerning many heart-lifting natural occurrences. Perhaps this is the logical way to define words, since human beings hold widely divergent opinions. But there ought to be a special category for spring rain. The succinct statement, "Water falling in drops condensed from vapor in the atmosphere," does less than justice to the blessing of a warm spring rain.

When the season has worked along to the point where green peas make colorful lines above the garden's brown soil and the rhubarb stalks are a foot high, a spring rain produces magical results. Meadows and sidehills that were predominantly brown suddenly turn green. Overnight the hardwoods put on pale green robes; the forsythias by the garden wall are banks of golden blooms. In perennial borders beneath farm kitchen windows, jonquils lift pennants of gold to the soft, steady rain.

Husbandmen stand in open barn doorways and watch the rain fall to earth. A spring rain in the city means splashes from speeding wheels and more difficulty in hailing a taxi. But out on the land where men live intimately with the weather, it is a welcome thing. The water fills wells and springs; it means nourishment in Earth's breast and the loosening of magic forces to start crops and grasses toward fulfillment.

There is no conclusion in Nature's cycle. The times of birth, growth, and rest blend imperceptibly into one another. When man's reckoning of time shows the approach of May and a spring rain blesses the countryside, he who is attuned to the heart lift of the seasons knows that even as the cold of winter must pass so in due time comes the season of new growth.

BASS DRUMMER

THE sonorous bass notes of the bullfrogs are heard in the land at the close of a spring day. The time of dusk signifies the opening of their evening concert from pond, stream, and swamp. There's something soothing and relaxing about the deep-pitched music. It's unhurried yet persistent. There's no tension or straining in it. The throaty, husky tones come across field and garden and drift into kitchen windows and barns where men are finishing their evening chores.

The bullfrog is an unusual creature. There are occasions when he resembles a miniature ogre from the region beyond the seven-times-circling Styx. His loose green skin is rough and wrinkled; it is cold and slippery to the touch. *Rana* has powerful hind legs that fit snugly against his body when he is sit-

6

ting on the brook's bank. Somehow those folded legs remind one of the retractable wheels of big bulky airplanes. Then again he looks like a wise, half-cynical, tolerant old man of the world as he lifts his head and cocks one of his huge, prominent eyes. There's a band of gleaming gold around the pupil and another around the outer margin. When "jug o' rum" winks, the nictitating membrane rises from below and covers the whole staring eye.

The bullfrogs bring a note of cheer to the countryman's heart when they emerge from their winter's sleep and start tuning up for their evening concerts. At the end of a spring day when night shadows are falling and stars are being lighted in the sky, their chorus adds a melodious accent to the quiet of the countryside and signifies the arrival of a new season.

HOT BISCUITS AND MAPLE SYRUP

THERE comes a time in the spring of the year when the countryman has a dish that rates superlatives in his customarily calm appraisal of foods. True, he can have the same dish at any season by judiciously storing a sufficiency of the ingredients for year-round needs. A farmer who knows the good flavors of earthborn products isn't at all averse to it in October or December. But when a man comes in from the chores on a spring evening, he walks a little faster through the ell when he's heard a rumor that hot biscuits and new maple syrup are scheduled for supper.

This dish is an example of harmonious partnership. It's as good a team as deep-dish apple pie and sharp cheese or hot

7

gingerbread and cottage cheese. There are, admittedly, biscuits and biscuits. First-class ones are as light as milkweed down; they are so hot that, when they are broken on a parallel plane, the fragrant steam rises in miniature clouds. The bottom crust is firm but flaky. The top crust is crisp, very short, and a rich brown that rivals the color of oak leaves after the heavy frosts of late autumn.

Plenty of golden, farm-churned butter should be spread on the opened biscuits, and then the golden syrup should be poured generously over them. This is a dessert rarely mentioned in cookbooks. It should be eaten while the biscuits are piping hot and the upper and bottom crusts are firm and crunchy. The logical vessel in which to serve it is a soup plate.

There are many heart-warming features about the spring season. The countryman who has hot biscuits and maple syrup for supper savors one of the best of them.

BAG MENDING

BEFORE men harnessed power to long assembly lines and whirring machinery tossed out completed products for myriad uses, good countrymen believed that a penny saved was a penny earned. "Waste not, want not" was a fundamental tenet on farms among the hills and in the valleys. At the turn of the century farmers in the Northeast still raised barley, oats, wheat, and field corn. In the fall after the threshing was done and the corn husked and shelled, it was common practice to take a load of grain in burlap bags to the local gristmill for grinding. Thus

8

it came to be, and it still is to a certain extent, an essential task on the farm to keep the burlap bags mended.

A city dweller might ask why the bags need to be mended. In spite of several cats and a dog, rats and mice abound wherever grain is stored, and they chew holes through the burlap. Therefore bag mending is an important link in the chain of tasks that constitute good husbandry.

There's an art to the work. After a spring rain, when the soil is too wet to be worked or the fields are too soft for spreading barnyard dressing, the countryman likes to sit on a wheelbarrow in the sunny yard or on a box in the barn doorway and ply the long needle attached to heavy thread. Small holes and rips are sewed together with crisscross darning stitches; they have to be reasonably close to prevent the ground grain from seeping through. Big holes and gashes are another matter. They must be mended with pieces from bags that have served their original purpose and are now sources of patching material. There's nothing spectacular about the task—it's just a homely, puttery job that has to be done. But after a spell of hard work, many a countryman rather enjoys sitting in the sun and catching up on his bag mending.

SPLITTING WOOD

SPLITTING wood is a task the countryman enjoys—and for several reasons. It is not one of the pressing seasonal jobs that is subject to the dictates of time. Naturally, after the wood is sawed, a man likes to get it split and wheelbarrowed into the shed before the rush of plowing, harrowing, and planting is upon him. But with this deadline several weeks away he can work along at a comfortable tempo and enjoy the deep satisfaction that comes with the readying of the fuel for another season.

The feel of his favorite ax is pleasant—an ax just the right heft and balance, with a razor-keen cutting edge. Men who split wood know that the secret of efficient work is not brute strength and weight. Splitting wood is an art that one learns by experience. There should be a big, solid chopping block, not too high, not too low, but just the right height to fit the chopper. Then when he brings the ax down, the piece to be split must be just the proper distance away to get the full power of the blow.

Each chunk of wood poses a separate problem. Each must be studied for the run of the grain. Clear pieces of oak and maple and birch split easily. It is when there are knots and twists that a man takes a minute to ponder. Some of the chunks of old apple wood and beech are too knotty to split for the kitchen range. These are tossed to a separate pile for use in the parlor base-burner. As the piles increase, the clean, bracing fragrance of split wood blends with the spicy pungency of the sawdust. There's time to rest a few minutes and listen to the high, haunting notes of the wood pewee that float down from the wood lot above the orchard. And if, by chance, the aroma of frying doughnuts comes from an open kitchen window, a man is never so pressed for time that he can't take a few minutes to see how the baking has turned out.

TO own a fringed-top surrey was a mark of distinction. It set one apart from the driver of the humble and useful two-seated democrat which not only would carry a family of six comfortably, but also, with the rear seat removed, would afford space for a barrel of apples or a few bags of potatoes when the family went to trade at the village store.

The fringed-top surrey was a different matter. It was a four-wheeled, two-seated pleasure carriage, and anything dedicated solely to pleasure was in a category by itself. The surrey was a lightweight wagon. Instead of a plain box body it had stylish cutouts before each seat; in the place of wooden frame seat-sides it had open grillwork. The dashboard was low and had a rakish, jaunty air.

The glory of the surrey, however, was its fringed top. That aristocratic canopy set it apart from everyday living. Supported on four steel rods, it gave a family protection from the sun. A man didn't use his surrey if it looked like rain. However, many of the surreys had rain curtains that were carried beneath the rear seat. They could, in emergencies, be buttoned inside the fringe at the top and to knobs along the outside of the body.

There were certain occasions when the surrey was used. On pleasant summer Sundays it took the family to church. On Fourth of July, on Old Home Day, and at the Wednesday evening band concerts it appeared in numbers. The black body with its narrow, red trim-line, the black-rimmed wheels, and the red spokes had a style that appealed. The surrey has gone, along with buckboards, top buggies, and democrats, but it was a symbol of good life on the farm a generation ago.

12

AT the turn of the century, thank-you-ma'ams were an important factor in the building of country roads. There has been a long-lasting and never-settled argument among countrymen as to the original purpose of thank-you-ma'ams. The pioneers who built the dirt roads that wind over the hills of the Northeast conscientiously constructed the humps. One school maintains that they were constructed so that oxen and horses could rest on the upgrades without having to hold the weight of their loads. The other claims that the ridges were built to carry off eroding water after torrential summer rainstorms. To date there seems to be no group which admits a combination of purposes—but it takes time to evolve workable compromises.

A good thank-you-ma'am is not placed carelessly or made hastily. The hill, especially if it has a curve, must be studied. The ridges must be so placed that water will be deflected before it has a chance to gain momentum. In a region where teams are still used, the mounds must be near enough together so that the horses will have a chance for a rest when they pull heavy loads. In those areas where farmers still have a chance to work on the road in the spring in return for the cancellation of part of their tax bill, men pride themselves on building a series of thank-you-ma'ams on a hill. The gullied hills are a reflection of their ability. Some demand hard-packed gravel bars; others believe a clay and gravel mixture is best.

It should be mentioned in passing that some countrymen insist that the correct name for the hillside humps is "Kiss-me-quick." Perhaps in those halcyon days of red-wheeled buggies, snappy roaders, and colorful buggy whips, there was some basis in fact for the name. Either way, those water-defying, team-resting bars have played an intriguing part in a nation's transportation system.

PUSSY WILLOWS

DOWN in the ravine sloughs, along the banks of meadow brooks and creeks, around the shores of ponds, and at the swamp's edge, the pussy willows are bursting the stitching that has held the bud scales tightly wrapped through the time of cold. The willow is one of the first members of the tree family to proclaim that a new season has arrived. While the snow is still deep in the evergreen woods and drifts of the packed granular whiteness shrink slowly in the shade on the north side of the barn, the glaucous willow flings its gray-furred pennants to the early April sunshine.

Rarely does the pussy willow grow to the stature of a tree. It is commonly found as a scraggly, irregular shrub a few feet tall, and its largest shoots are not more than an inch or two in diameter. Although it is neither pretentious nor particularly handsome in itself, it brings beauty to the countryside while the landscape is still sear and brown. The soft, pollen-bearing catkins have a beautiful yellow sheen at the height of their bloom. On a sunny day one finds the queen bumblebees clambering over the blossoms, collecting the nectar that means another brood is about to be started in a small ground-anchored nest. The seed-bearing catkins develop small pointed fruits that break open in early summer and release downy seeds which drift away on the wind.

14

For a brief interlude, while the buds on the maples, birches, and beeches are starting their swelling toward fruition, the pussy willows bring beauty to the watercourses and the edges of moist places. The willows have been called the despair of botanists because, in addition to nearly two hundred recognized species, there are innumerable natural hybrids. But the countryman isn't concerned over the technical aspects of the situation. He knows that when the willows open their buds and the plump gray dots make patterns in the sunshine, a new season is at hand.

BUCKWHEATS

THERE may be differences of opinion regarding current needs, but high on the countryman's list is more and better buckwheats for breakfast. Some people insist on calling them griddle cakes, but any old-timer who knows what "start the batter the day before you use it" means, will agree that "griddle cake" is not the proper name to apply to the best breakfast dish yet devised by the mind of man. People with dainty appetites who sip a cup of coffee and nibble a thin slice of overtoasted bread will not be interested in this morning-brightening, pioneer-proved food that clings to the ribs until the noon whistle.

Although good cooks often vary in their methods, we countrymen are arbitrary about buckwheats. This business of pouring ready-mixed material into a bowl, adding some water, and calling the resulting mass "buckwheat batter" violates all the articles of *Fagopyrum's* bill of rights. Good buckwheat batter requires time to mellow and age to just the right degree of ripeness. Sometime during the forenoon, buckwheat flour, salt, warm water, and yeast should be put in a heavy stone jar. Let the mixture stand in a warm place overnight. Keep the jar covered with a plate. The next morning measure some baking soda into a few tablespoonfuls of boiling water, mix thoroughly with the batter, and the buckwheats are ready for the hot greased griddle.

Some countrymen put molasses on buckwheats; there are areas where human beings eat milk gravy on the round, brown disks. Without being unduly dogmatic, however, there's only one way to eat buckwheats. Stack four or five on a big plate; put a generous quantity of butter between each layer and a little extra on top; then over the whole pour a cupful or two of golden maple syrup. That's what our ancestors meant by buckwheats.

CHIMNEY SWIFT

THE chimney swift dresses in a sooty-black cloak and grayish waistcoat. In repose, he's an unimpressive chap with a very wide mouth and a very short beak. He catches his food as he flies through the air. His name is well bestowed, for he's been clocked flying 110 miles an hour. His home is a messy, helter-skelter affair—a sort of open pocket made with small sticks nearly equal in length and size and stuck fast to the chimney wall by a gluey saliva that the birds secrete. For many years it was a mystery where *Chaetura pelagica* went during the winter months; now the Wildlife Service has traced him to hidden valleys in Peru during the cold period in the North.

These are prosaic facts. When the sun sinks low and shadows creep across the fields and meadows, it's time for the swifts' aerial circus. They put on a breath-taking and beautiful exposition of graceful flying as they climb and dive, circle and swoop. Like a team of miniature airplanes they fill the air with their stunts. Every few minutes one of the birds, his mouth filled with insects, hovers hesitatingly over the chimney top and suddenly drops out of sight. Then up he comes, gains speed with the zip of jet propulsion, and is off through the air, swooping and darting and turning, accumulating another load for the babies in the stick-woven nest.

When darkness settles over the countryside and the farmer comes in from his last look at the livestock in the barn, he hears the murmurings and twitterings in the chimneys as the swifts settle for the night. Gradually the bird talk ceases and the farmstead quiets for the hours of darkness. All is well with the friendly chimney dwellers.

FIFTH MONTH'S URGENCY

MAY is the month when husbandmen hasten to prepare the soil and to plant seeds, confident that sun and moisture will work their mysterious processes and that in good time Earth will yield her bounties for the needs of man. In the countryside patient horses plod up and down the fields. Long ribbons of moist brown soil curl away from the glistening share and lie in symmetrical patterns as chugging tractors wheel back and forth, speeding the work for men who must labor in accord with the season's fullness.

The leaves on beeches, oaks, maples, and birches are pushing outward and upward. The poplars, alders, and willows are giant grayish-green bouquets. The sumac buds have begun to swell on the scraggly, twisted branches. The old gaunt Sheldon pear tree behind the woodshed is a mass of white blossoms. The slender stalks of the peach trees on the south slope are long pennants of pink.

From the brown carpet of the woodland the wake-robins, painted trilliums, and lady's-slippers are lifting green stalks upward to the mullioned shafts of light. The brook-traversed meadows have pushed their new grasses above the frost-tanned winter growth, and the upthrusting buds of the cowslips are growing plumper each day. In swamps and on rocky hillsides the small rose-purple blossoms of the high-bush blueberries are open to the May sun. Gone now is the creeping advance of Earth's first awakening. This is the crescendo movement of her annual symphony.

THE flicker is an extrovert. On an exhilarating spring day when the bluebirds, wood pewees, and song sparrows are singing a melodious trio arrangement, goldenwing callously interrupts with his loud, monotonous performance. There's little musical quality to his song; his dogmatic and self-assured notes repeat themselves for long periods. One who is close enough can catch the short grace note that precedes the steady-toned repetition of the main theme.

He has a score of folklore names, such as highhole, yellowhammer, yaccer, and woodwall. It's always a joyous occasion in spring when the countryman hears that familiar and aggressive string of rasping notes from the old Baldwin orchard behind the barn. The flicker wants the countryside to know that he has arrived and has everything under control. Goldenwing earned his nickname because of the yellow that shows beneath his tail and wings when in flight. But if he had no yellow feathers he would still be a handsome bird. He wears a bright red scarf on the back of his neck; he has a gray topknot and a deep black mustache that runs from the corners of his mouth to the red band. His throat is a tawny grayish brown and his waistcoat has a crescent-shaped black ruffle.

He and his demure mate usually choose a deep hole in an apple tree for housekeeping. She lays five to eight pure-white eggs and, after the chicks are hatched, tends assiduously to business. Goldenwing, to give him credit, does help with the food hunting and brings quantities of grubs, ants, and worms to his hungry family. However, he's never too busy in the early part of the season to take time out for his song. He's a fellow who knows just what he wants and acts as if he expected to get it. No doubts, questionings, or conferences are necessary so far as he is concerned. All in all he's a welcome member of the wildlife family.

THE GREENERY PROBLEM

A PERUSAL of contemporary home magazines and the food pages of today's papers leads one to the conclusion that the time has arrived when men must get together and take a firm stand on an important problem. The matter of greenery masquerading as food has gone far enough. It's getting so that every time a man has a steak, a chop, or a dish of good plebeian mashed potatoes set before him, he has to spend a quarter hour picking off the parsley.

There's nothing intrinsically wrong with parsley. If the womenfolks want to eat the aromatic garden herb, there isn't anything in our form of representative democratic government to prevent them. If they want to chop it up and use it in soups and stews, that's all right—if they don't use too much. One readily concedes that on the basis of available evidence, green feed is good for cows, chickens, and rabbits. Who is Homo sapiens to insist that what is good for his animals is not beneficial to him?

But it's being overdone. A mess of lettuce leaves and gelatinous matter topped with a red cherry and the whole smeared with whipped cream or some form of dressing isn't nourishing

21

fare. This nation was built from a wilderness on honest food. Perhaps it's too much to expect a platter of fried salt pork, milk gravy, and boiled potatoes very often. Dried apple pies and triple-layer chocolate cakes have gone out of fashion. Homemade bread and fried mush belong to the past, along with fringe-topped surreys and high button shoes. But if all good men will come to the aid of the cause, there's a fighting chance of stopping this greenery business before it goes too far.

PLANTING BY THE MOON

THIS is a scientific age, and the learned men who delve in retorts and test tubes are no doubt justified in their opinions. The planting of seeds is a sacred task, and the farmer who labors to prepare a mellow seedbed does so with confidence that time, sun, and rain will bring forth the harvest. Through the centuries husbandmen have toiled in the faith that as a man sows so shall he reap. Science says simply that when the earth is warm, moist, and in good tilth—that is the time to sow seed.

But there are those who believe another factor is essential. A countryman who uses the help of science in every way possible—except for determining the time of planting—takes a look at the *Old Farmer's Almanac* and waits until the moon is right. The belief has been transmitted through the years that crops which mature below the surface should be planted in the dark of the moon or during the period of waning, while crops which fruit above should be planted while the moon waxes or is nearing fullness.

The Department of Agriculture announced long ago that

22

"moon farming" had no scientific basis. Many farmers, however, still believe that if the moon can control the tides of the oceans it can influence the action of soil. There is much to be learned about the mysteries of plant growth, and perhaps in years to come something will be discovered that relates to seed germination in connection with the moon's phases. Meanwhile the countryman who works with Nature calmly studies his *Almanac* and waits. Science is his friend, but experience has been his teacher. He remembers that scientists proved that airplanes and horseless carriages were impracticable a few decades ago. For long years the waxing and waning of the moon has been a good and dependable guide. It's natural, therefore, for him to pay it a certain allegiance.

MAY MELODIES

MAY is the prime of spring, the heyday of the period that bridges the gap between winter and summer. There are days when the sun's heat rests on the countryside, and one is sure that the Weather Man has mixed his dates. Then comes a day or two of chilly rain, and the countryman can feel in the raw air the last lingering touches of winter's cold.

In the main, the fifth month is one of the year's loveliest, and many people unhesitatingly state it is their favorite. May is a month of melody. When the first faint fingers of dawn begin to caress the earth, the birds of garden, field, and wood tune their voices for the morning symphony that welcomes the day. It's a stirring theme the glee club flings to an awakening world as the sun's slanting rays pierce the lifting mists—a hallelujah chorus that proclaims the very heart of springtime.

But the music has an even deeper meaning. It hails the new season as Earth responds to its ecstasy and begins her progress toward the time of fruition. Hilltop trees that have stood like sharply limned etchings against the sky are taking on their summer raiment. Shrubs and bushes along the brooks and creeks are once more solid masses of green; old zigzag rail fences again become half-camouflaged, and the wild folk use them for sanctuary. Each day the sun circles higher and the dusks grow longer.

When day is done and thin gray shadows begin to inch across the landscape, the evening chorus begins. At either end of the span of daylight hours in May the birds make music. As gray dusk deepens to night's blackness, the bird symphony diminuendoes to the last few sleepy calls from the woodland's edge. This is May—the month of melody.

MARCHING EVERGREENS

IF the countryman gets off the main arteries onto the quiet country roads that wind back among the hills and beside small mountain valleys, he will see the marching evergreens. The serried ranks of the dark-hued trees stride down the steep slopes of thin-soiled upland pastures. They step forward year by year across the ledge-laced shoulders of foothill mountains. They plod steadily ahead on sidehill mowings and edge their way into the rich meadow land.

A century and more ago pioneering farmers came into these hills and established homes. A good farm needed both lowland

and upland. Through the decades additional land was cleared for grass, grains, and pasture. Stump fences with tangled roots, zigzag split-rail boundaries, and gray granite walls marked the limits of man's subjugation of Nature. Trees, bracken, and brush were torn from Earth's breast. Man took violent dominion of what he desired.

Then the fertile, stone-free soil of the West called; industries in cities and towns beckoned. One by one the farms back in the hills were abandoned. With confident patience Nature bided her time. Now the evergreens are on the march. Each season the tall hemlocks, pines, firs, and spruces in the rear ranks loose their winged seeds. Each spring the miracle of birth is reenacted in the vanguard. Tiny spikes of pale green start upward to sun and light, taking their places in the ever-forming ranks. Year by year the marching army moves forward. Nature never hurries. For thousands of years before the white man came the trees possessed the land. Now that the farms are reverting to the wilderness, the trees will again take possession. There's poignant appeal in the story of the striding green ranks to anyone who is sensitive to the drama of his country's growth.

FEEDING THE HENS

IT's different now. Hens are kept in multidecked apartment houses. It's taken for granted that the feathered ladies shall have running water, electric lights, air conditioning, and a scientifically concocted ration that includes just the right amounts of proteins, fats, and carbohydrates, as well as all the necessary vitamins.

26

There was a time when the countryman considered hens essential but simple members of the farm's livestock. He granted they were somewhat temperamental; he conceded they possessed only moderate intelligence. Each spring a few hens were set on clutches of eggs in the quiet dimness under the north scaffold of the horse barn, and in due time the clucking, fussy mothers wandered around the farmyard with their broods. A good farmer liked to have plenty of fryers for summer and roasters for fall, plus a batch of pullets for layers.

Feeding the hens in those unscientific days was a simple task. When chore time came, a lad took a wooden measure, filled it with whole corn, oats, and barley in the grain room and never had a worry about vitamins or nutritional balance. As he stepped from the barn and started in the direction of the hencoop, the birds came running toward him from all directions. There was a confused, high-pitched babel of voices—similar to the noises made by all forms of animal life, high or low, when food is in the offing. It was fun to take handfuls of the clean, hard grains and scatter them widely so all the hens could get a fair share, for there are bullies and selfish ones, social gradations and inhibitions in hen society as well as in human society. Feeding the hens was a pleasant day's-end task. As a lad listened to the excited, hungry talk change to a low, contented murmur, he glimpsed the fundamental importance of food in life's scheme.

THIS tall, coarse herb with spreading leaves and thick, succulent stalks is one of the harbingers of spring. Men may differ of course in their opinions as to its most efficacious use. Rhubarb pie has a large following. Another group of articulate adherents lobbies persistently for cold rhubarb sauce covered with thick cream. A third school of commendable perspicacity and judicial discrimination knows the satisfying goodness of rhubarb pudding served with cream that's been delicately sweetened with just a whiffle of maple syrup.

The countryman has given time and thought to the problem, and it is his considered judgment that, of the three, he prefers a deep-dish, tangy, juicy rhubarb pie. During the season, he eats it with all three meals, and a leftover piece or two amalgamates pleasantly with a glass of cold creamy milk for a bedtime snack.

A rhubarb pie must be made leisurely, calmly, and philosophically, in full cognizance of the importance of the task. A deplorable number of ladies skip certain vital processes. The lower crust must be lined to a depth of three-sixteenths of an inch with a mixture of sugar and flour. Never peel rhubarb for an honest pie. (If it's that leathery, make a sauce.) Use a deep plate and gently round the filling before the top crust goes on. Don't be afraid to toss a modicum of flour over the pieces of edible stem. Use a handy tool to puncture the top crust so the juices and steam will have an avenue of escape. Dot the crust with pieces of butter and shake on a smidgen of cinnamon. When a man tops off his meal with a couple of wedges of correctly made rhubarb pie, the alarms of a jittery world fall into proper perspective.

THE humble, old-fashioned purple lilac is part of our national tradition. When brought to this country about the middle of the seventeenth century, it already had a long and interesting history. It came from Persia to Constantinople in the twelfth or thirteenth century, and traveled slowly across Europe to England. In his *Garden of Pleasante Flowers,* which was written in 1629, Parkinson called the purple lilac "the blew pipe tree."

Over wide areas of our nation its fragrant masses of bloom bring cheer in the spring. Its thick deep green leaves hold their sheen through the heat and drought of midsummer. There are clumps of *Syringa vulgaris* growing in old stonewall-lined cemeteries in New England; it stands faithful guard over the sacred spots where courageous pioneers lie sleeping across a continent. As home-seeking men and women pushed over mountains, across rivers, and through shoulder-high prairie grasses, they carried roots of the lilac with them. No one has a complete record of the things mothers and wives tucked into the Conestoga wagons and prairie schooners, but because man does not live by bread alone, lilacs, peonies, and favorite herbs blazed a trail along the virgin paths to new homes.

In Cornwall and Devon the maidens believe that dew from lilac blossoms will bring beauty to those who bathe their faces in it. Legends and folklore have accumulated about it in England's border country. In this nation it is a shrub associated with homemaking and with memorials to those who have gone before. Unpretentious and plain, it grows in gardens and by the corners of old cellar holes deep in woods that have reclaimed their own. Birds nest in its security and small wild folk seek sanctuary in its tangled dimness. The purple lilac has been a good companion to man as he has hewed a nation of homes from a wilderness.

STORE PORCH

SOME day a historian may write a history of the nation in terms of porches on general country stores. Research has failed to divulge the man of trade who first built a porch across the front of his store for the general benefit of his customers, but for a long time now, in hamlet, village, and town, a store porch has been an integral part of the scene Americana.

Since we have been preeminently a nation of trade and industry for well over half a century, it must be that a store porch fosters good will in business. The pattern is heart-warmingly similar in the East, South, North, and West. The porch is not too wide and the floor boards are old and weather-beaten. There are a few battered, more or less decrepit chairs; there is usually a box or two standing on end. Along the front there may be a wooden rail where in years gone by farmers tied their horses when they came in to trade. On the outside wall are gaudy-colored signs advocating the virtues of chewing tobaccos, pipe tobaccos, baking sodas, coffees, teas, horse liniments, calf medicines, and tonics for that run-down feeling. All this is an accepted and expected part of the environment.

But the store porch is more than this. It is a town meeting in miniature—a free and democratic forum where a man can express his convictions. One of its pleasant aspects is that whatever the proposition proposed there is always someone to take

the opposite side. National and international problems are settled with comforting finality; local road conditions and school appropriations can always be relied upon as subjects if, by a miracle, the world at large is fairly quiet for a few hours. But as long as men can sit on a store porch and say what they think, the nation is in a wholesome condition.

STACKING WOOD

A FARM lad of a dozen years or so is always deeply concerned over what Saturday will bring forth in the way of a task. If the weather is favorable in spring, a fellow is pretty sure of what Father will announce on a Saturday after breakfast. But if it is rainy, or if the soil is wet from a recent rain so that cultivating, planting, or hoeing are out of the picture, a boy feels some trepidation. Therefore, it is with a certain feeling of relief that he hears, "Well, Son, what do you say you stack wood today?" Stacking wood is not necessarily an exciting job, but it is far higher on the scale than sprouting potatoes or cleaning out the henhouse or the calf pen.

Before oil and electricity became common, a good farmer took pride in his woodpile. It took many cords to keep the big kitchen range and the parlor base-burner supplied during the year. After the pile was sawed and split in early spring, it became a boy's task to use the wheelbarrow and take the wood to the woodshed for stacking.

There is something appealing about an old woodshed. The floor is deep with litter-bits of wood, bark, sawdust, and debris. There is a peculiarly satisfying smell to it—a dry, acrid, pungent aroma compounded of dust and the different varieties of wood. Load after load comes in, and one carefully builds the tiers higher and higher. The splintery pieces of hardwood have to be fitted against each other so the tier will be firm and solid. The big, gnarled, knotty chunks for the parlor burner go into a heap in one corner; small stuff for kindling goes into another. And, of course, along about ten o'clock or so, if a young man smells the spicy, tantalizing fragrance of hot gingerbread or the bland, inviting aroma of freshly fried doughnuts, it is taken for granted that he will go to the kitchen to see how Mother is coming along with the Saturday baking.

Stacking wood is just one of the routine farm tasks, but when chore time arrives, a countryman takes pleasure at day's end in the sight of the good fuel ready for future use.

JUNE

STAND in a field of red clover or in a meadow starred with daisies and buttercups in June, and you can see, hear, and feel the high tide of the year coming to the land. There are many people who believe that June is the month of deepest appeal in the cycling seasons. There is a fresh green cloak on the landscape—a green still vivid with spring's growth. Each heart-lifting day, the sun climbs closer to the pole of the horizon.

On brown fields long, regularly spaced lines of green spears push from the warm earth and begin reaching upward to the sun. The rush of plowing and planting is over, and the husbandmen are nurturing crops toward the time of fruition. June is the month of cultivation. Tractors chug-chug through the long hours; big farm horses plod patiently up and down the rows. Small green balls hang from fruiting twigs, and the winged seeds of maples float gently down to earth. At dawn the birds' symphony makes music in the air. Through the heart of day the barn swallows swoop and circle, climb and dive, phoebes call from the roof of the woodshed, and song sparrows throw their carols to the sky from fence posts. Bees make humming music as they dart from flower to flower, fulfilling the commands of instinct that tell them to prepare for the long rest ahead.

June is high twelve in Nature's calendar. When day draws to a close and the sun dips from sight, the long quiet dusk brings its own beauty. Night's curtain is pulled slowly. The

35

last sleepy calls of robins sound in the semidarkness. The chimney swifts end their aerial circus. The haunting, lonesome call of the whippoorwill comes across the field. A June day has ended.

WILD STRAWBERRIES

MR. WEBSTER defines the strawberry as "the juicy, edible, usually red fruit of a genus (*Fragaria*) of rosaceous plants." To dismiss wild strawberries thus summarily is less than justice. William Butler was nearer the correct degree of enthusiasm when he remarked, "Doubtless God could have made a better berry, but doubtless God never did." When the gallant Duke of Gloucester, later Richard the Third, was discussing coronation plans with his lords, it is reported from no less a source than Shakespeare's *Richard III* that he asked the Bishop of Ely to send for some of them from his garden in Holborn.

The countryman looks ahead to several generous messes. There's something about wild-strawberry time that sets it apart as a special season on the calendar. Those who live in the country know the spots where they grow best; on the sunny slopes of upland pastures, on the grassy banks of ravines, in the upper mowing fields, and along the south sides of stone walls. Where a few weeks ago there was a profusion of white flowers with golden centers, now the tiny fruits are pointed in shape and deep crimson in color.

No matter how pressing the farm work, the countryman can spare an hour or two. With two-quart lard pails for containers, he is glad to do the picking. Of course when the pails are full, he is happy to turn them over to Mother and the girls for hulling. The point is: he knows that about a pint of the red nuggets, well crushed and poured over a couple of generously buttered homemade biscuits in a soup plate, will be waiting for him when he comes in from the evening chores. The countryman, facing his heaped plate with understandable anticipation, is certain they are the best of Nature's many free gifts of fields and forest.

LILLIPUTIAN KNIGHT

THE ruby-throated hummingbird is a tiny, fearless knight of the feathered world. Ordinarily he's a friendly, flashing sprite, seeking the nectar of flowers and blooming shrubs. But in the never-ceasing tournament of the bird world in which each male stakes out his claim to a certain area, *Trochilus colubris* can become a desperate duelist. Without asking odds or favors, he lunges with his slender, pointed blade at the enemy's breast. It may be that other birds realize his dauntless fighting spirit, for one seldom sees the rubythroat involved in warfare.

To watch a hummingbird in action is to observe the poetry of motion. One moment he is hovering in the honeysuckle or clematis by the porch; an instant later he is suspended before the spikes of delphiniums or larkspur. He is the helicopter of the bird world. In a flash he darts from a stationary position to any direction of the compass; up, down, or sideways, he handles himself efficiently and with lightning speed.

His nest is one of the loveliest in the bird world, a small, lichen-covered home high on a horizontal limb. Lined with bits of fluff from cattails and with the fronds of ferns, it looks like a natural excrescence on the branch. Two tiny white eggs fill the nest, and within a week from the time they are hatched, the new knights are ready to try their wings.

The rubythroat is native only to the New World and is one of the most colorful representatives of his family. With his bright metallic-green coat and the splash of red on his throat, he is a familiar and welcome friend around the home and garden.

MOUNTAIN LAUREL

WHEN the colonists began to clear the woodlands for their homes and farms, they came upon a shrub with lustrous green leaves that they believed was a variety of the laurel tree so common in England. It was natural that they called it after the home-country shrub. As time went on and the pioneers grew accustomed to its beautiful blossoms, someone with imagination thought that the blossoming plant looked as though it were covered with a profusion of colorful scraps of calico, and today in certain areas it is called "calico bush." Early settlers made wooden spoons from the matured branches to stir the boiling sorghum in their big iron kettles, so "spoon-wood" became another name for American mountain laurel, *Kalmia latifolia*.

Laurel in bloom is a carpet of loveliness laid for a time over the thin soil of a rocky hillside, pasture slope, or craggy ravine.

It's a magic rug in the shady places where trees or overhanging hills throw dim shadows during part of the day. The five-lobed pink or white saucer-shaped flowers with purple dots cluster at the ends of twisting, sturdy branches. Framed by the glossy, rich, dark green leaves, the total effect is a bouquet of exquisite beauty.

From Maine to Georgia and westward to Ohio, the calico bush is a part of the beauty of spring. Birds delight in its tangled security; small wild folk find shelter in its dark recesses. Mountain laurel, strong growing, ever green and generous with its loveliness, is one of Nature's good gifts to man.

TURNING THE GRINDSTONE

OLD worn grindstones in weather-grayed frames sit through the years behind corncribs, milk houses, and woodsheds. Successive generations of young men have turned the rusty iron cranks that whirl the smooth-grained stones against the scythes and cutter blades of mowing bars. Many a lad has felt the countryman was unconscionably fussy about getting a razor-sharp edge on his tools. Somehow a twelve-year-old on the end of a crank gives everyone a smile, except the future citizen furnishing the muscle power.

Not so long ago the grass of lush meadows and thin-soiled upland fields was cut by men who went forth in the early morning with scythes and snaths. Then farm lads had a real job to do when it came to turning the grindstone. Each man had two or three scythes to use for the forenoon's work. Today whirling gears furnish power for the mowing machines, but men still use the steel blades and bent wooden handles to trim the grass by walls and fences, around gardens, and along creeks and brooks.

Round and round and round a boy pushes the crank. From a tin can with a small hole in the bottom, drops of water fall rhythmically onto the stone. Carefully, methodically, and unhurriedly Father moves the blade back and forth. Sometimes when there's a nick in the steel and firm pressure has to be applied, a lad must grit his teeth and exert his strength to keep up the momentum. From time to time Father lifts the scythe and leisurely tests the edge with the ball of his thumb. Then a lad has to decide whether to take a few moments rest or to keep the heavy stone whirling.

On a pleasant morning when a young man has woodchuck holes to explore and the trout are waiting in the pasture brook, turning the grindstone seems an interminable task. Come summer days, men who are far removed from the countryside of their youth, look out of the windows and remember the long-ago days when they turned the old grindstone.

BIRCH SWINGING

THERE is something about birch swinging that puts it in a class by itself as a form of entertainment. Jungle gyms, see-saws, swings from a tree branch, and jumps from a high scaffold into the haymow all have their points. But when a twelve-year-old lad is going for the cows in the late afternoon and comes to a clump of white or gray birches, he will naturally take time out for a few minutes of Tarzan-like recreation.

There is a technique to birch swinging that a chap learns by experience. In the first place, the tree must be the right size. A slender fifteen-footer bends over too quickly. A fellow does not get more than eight or ten feet off the ground before the tree goes over, oftentimes with disconcerting suddenness. A few solid jars as he hits Mother Earth convince him that he had better go higher and come down more slowly.

A twenty-footer is just about right if a boy wants to be certain of results. It is sturdy enough so he can climb nearly to the top. It bends with a degree of strength behind it that is reassuring as he dangles in the air. Sometimes, of course, one makes a mistake in sizing up the situation. The tree bends over, but not far enough. Then, if legs are kicking wildly in the air and the top half is nearly horizontal with the ground, there are a few moments of uncertainty. But usually by swinging up and down in rhythmic motion, one can come nearer the ground each time until it is safe to let go.

The biggest thrill is climbing a twenty-five-footer and swinging in the air without thought of going low enough to drop to the ground. On a day when there is a stiff wind blowing, it is almost like flying. The top bends over, but one is still ten or even fifteen feet from the ground. One sways back and forth, up and down. Sometimes there are alarming creaks and groans. Then, still clinging by his hands, a lad has to work himself back to where he can get his legs around the trunk. A few scratches and a rip or two in his pants are taken for granted. Birch swinging is an adventure—and good adventures always take a toll.

THE era of the parlor organ was a substantial period in our country's development. It was a fitting musical accompaniment to the decades that featured buffalo robes, high button shoes, and fringed-top surreys. It is good to know that there is a brisk demand for pianos today. There is also a place in the home for flutes, clarinets, slide trombones, and snare drums in the hands of vigorous young people. But the parlor organ used to have distinctive qualities because it featured group interest instead of individual effort.

It sat in a corner of the room, with the upholstery on the stool matching the covering on the pedals. When Mother played the organ on a Sunday evening and the whole family gathered around to sing familiar hymns and the timeless home songs, the music made its mark in hearts and minds. Father enjoyed adding his bass. Boys and girls sang the melody and learned by ear the meaning of harmony.

Mother could perform minor miracles with the stops. She used deep diapason for the bass of "Carry Me Back to Old Virginny" and added forte for "When the Roll Is Called Up Yonder." Young folks watched as she pulled out dulciana and aeoline for the sweet, haunting melody of "Swanee River" and "Flow Gently, Sweet Afton." The songs sung at home were the same ones used in schools and at Grange and vestry Socials, so when friends were in for an evening, each person knew the words of every stanza.

The parlor organ is a humble instrument compared with a piano. But there are homes today where hands still change vox jubilante, flute d'amour, subbass, and salicional to suit the tempo and mood of "Annie Laurie," "Clementine," and "Three Blind Mice." Boys and girls of a generation ago sang around the organ and gained much from the experience. Its rich full tones were a part of the symphony that marked a happy home.

R.F.D. BOXES

SOME day a historian will write a chronicle of country living in terms of the R.F.D. boxes that stand like exclamation points along hundreds of thousands of miles of roads. No one who lives in cities and towns where the gray-uniformed man trudges up to the door and deposits the mail once or twice a day can fully appreciate the meaning of the R.F.D. box on a country road three or four miles from the village.

It is a cosmopolitan sort of box with a range of style as comprehensive as the fashions that adorn milady's tresses. There are some R.F.D. receptacles that will hold half a bushel of newspapers, magazines, and bulky mail-order catalogues. On these roomy boxes that sit on posts before big, prosperous-looking homes, one often sees the name of the farm in red letters. In the last few years, Art with a capital "A" has come to the rural-free-delivery containers. Some of them are replicas of bungalows and birdhouses; others are copies of old-time stage coaches. A current favorite is a reproduction of a covered wagon pulled by a pair of red-and-white oxen.

But the real, genuine, honest-to-goodness R.F.D. box is a humble, everyday sort of affair. It is rectangular with a curved top to shed rain and sleet. It has a small red metal flag that

44

goes up to tell the mailman a letter is waiting for him. If he leaves something in the box, he also raises the flag. The box sits on a weathered, splintery post by the side of the road.

Through the plebeian gray box have passed some of the heartbeats of a nation. Farm boys and girls write to the cities for the things that interest them. The family far from urban centers writes to the mail-order houses for both personal and farm necessities. Boys and girls, who have left the farm to seek the trail of life's adventures in distant cities, write letters home. The mail box sitting beside the country road is a link in the chain that binds a nation into one people.

ROCKING CHAIRS

THE time has come when good men should unite to stem the rush of waters over cherished and traditional concepts of comfort. There is logic in streamlining kitchens into compact food-preparation laboratories. Plate-glass windows are all right. If people cannot see enough from the regular-sized windows, picture windows have their points. If the ladies find lace curtains too great a chore, a man can accept the idea that rows of slats will be the mid-century style in window draperies.

When it is suggested, however, that rocking chairs are an outmoded relic of the preatomic age, the time has come to make a stand. A correctly made rocker, big enough to relax in comfortably, with rockers that permit a man to sway gently back and forth without danger of a rear overturn, is one of the most functional pieces of funiture ever devised. In years past there were a goodly number of choices if a new rocker were

45

needed. Some were broad and low, with upholstered seats. Others were all wood, good solid maple or birch, stained a deep cherry red or a rich mahogany brown. Mother always wanted her Boston rocker when she had a few minutes to rest during the day and for the long comfortable hours on winter evenings.

The greatest danger in current ideology concerns the future of the porch on summer evenings. It was distressing enough when the old swinging hammock was superseded by modern contraptions of metal that glide back and forth in a six-inch sway. But if the householder after a day's work cannot sit in a big wicker rocker on his porch and enjoy the evening, something will be lost. There are so many uncontrolled alarms and diversions in the world today that a man needs the gentle soporific movement of a favorite rocking chair to keep his balance.

GOING FOR THE COWS

GOING for the cows in the late afternoon is one of the tasks that a twelve-year-old likes. It is just possible, however, that going for the cows is not, per se, the entire story. After a lad has been cultivating potatoes or corn for several hours, or by some evil fate has had to thin the carrots or pick a bushel or two of peas, it is welcome news when Father glances at his watch and says, "Well, Son, about time to get the cows."

The young man whistles for Shep, the farm collie, who has been dozing on the cool earth in the tool shed. Together they set out down the rutted lane from the barnyard to the pasture.

Shep insists on a careful exploration of the woodchuck's hole under the stone wall, and a lad likes to study the sharply etched chuck's footprints in the moist brown earth. In the clump of alders at the end of the lane where a catbird has its nest, the gray-coated mimic slips away and calls impatiently from the high-bush cranberry clump at the edge of the field.

The pasture is studded with daisies, buttercups, clusters of juniper, sheep laurel, and sprawling mats of wild pasture roses. A boy takes a peek at the field sparrow's nest he discovered the other day. The little fellows are about ready to leave. If he is lucky, he may see the dainty footprints of a red fox where he was investigating the chances of capturing a field mouse.

A young man knows how long it is safe to dawdle. Then he rounds up the cows and, with Shep at their heels, starts them homeward. The cows need no driving. They would not start voluntarily of course, but when they see that he is ready, they go along. As the cows follow the deep ruts worn smooth by half a century of summer travel, a lad can dream of important things—a new jackknife, the book on trapping in the northland, and the big trout in the meadow pool. Going for the cows is one of the more satisfying tasks on a farm.

PITCHING HORSESHOES

WE are glad there is a national association to guide officially the destinies of pitching horseshoes. If the people who enjoy projecting arrows from semicircular pieces of wood or knocking around an inoffensive wooden ball have organizations behind them, then those who pitch horseshoes deserve the dignity of similar treatment.

A game after supper on the farm, however, needs no official sanction. Two deeply driven stakes of oak or ash forty feet apart and a few old horseshoes are all the equipment needed. A man who pitches regularly is particular about his "shoes." They can be neither too heavy nor too light. They must feel right in a man's hands. The countryman who enjoys the game from April to December is just as fussy about his prize pair of old horseshoes as he is about his favorite ax or his pet hoe.

One of the pleasant things about pitching horseshoes is the diversity of opinion regarding the techniques—and that's the way it should be in a democracy where one's opinion is respected among one's peers. Some men insist that a ringer comes easier from holding the shoe by the calk at the rear center and letting the shoe go three times end over end. Others maintain that one end-over-end revolution is best. There are those who stoutly argue the only proper way is to hold the shoe sideways, with a thumb curled around a front calk. Others balance the shoe on several fingers and figure that two and three-quarters turns will produce the most ringers.

These arguments of course, are merely the technicalities of a blood-stirring, traditional American sport. For some three centuries men and boys have been exercising their skill with the pieces of curved iron. It's the good-natured rivalry, the masculine banter, and the pitting of one's skill against another's that gives zest to pitching horseshoes. When the shout "It's a ringer!" comes, a man has a feeling that he's accomplished something worth while.

GOOD OLD SUMMERTIME

WHEN a countryman takes a little nooning in the shade of the tree at the house corner on a July day and looks out over the heat-blanketed fields, meadows, and pastures he's apt to recall the familiar phrase, "the good old summertime." In spite of certain discomforts it is a good season of the year.

There's a spirit of tranquillity and brooding fulfillment over the land. The sun hangs like a molten golden ball in the blue sky. Barn swallows swoop and wheel over the fields; catbirds scold from the hedge around the garden, and deep in the woods a crow sends forth his melancholy, halfhearted call. In the heat of noontime, the cows gather under a clump of trees and wait for the sun to lower before grazing again. The hens congregate beneath the tangle of blackberry vines and dust themselves in cool holes in the earth.

One can almost see the corn push higher day by day, and the kitchen garden is lush with greenery. Along the brushy lines of walls and rail fences the quail rest in the shade and wait for the cool of evening. The plump, philosophical toads burrow in the moist earth beneath the tomato and melon vines.

And then in the evening, after a day's work in the hot sun, the countryman sits in his favorite rocker on the porch and watches day turn into night. The swallows dart through the air; the robins carol their evening song. And as dusk gradually turns into darkness, fireflies dot the night with red gleams while frogs chant their monotone symphony. It's a good time of year, a part of Nature's cycle when the promises of spring are finding fruition in plant and animal life.

THE Algonquins had a name for the hemlock. They called it "Oh-neh-tah," meaning "Green-on-the-stick." The hemlock does not have the calm, self-contained dignity of the white pine; it does not pretend to match the crisp, sturdy beauty of the resinous spruce. Nor does it offer the fragile loveliness of the wispy firs. *Tsuga canadensis* is the humble cousin of the evergreen family. That is why it is so fitting that the hemlocks and gray birches often keep each other company on thin-soiled stretches of rocky uplands, in cold swamps, and on the sandy sides of ravines. The gray birch is the Martha of its family, too.

The countryman is partial to the stands of hemlocks. He enjoys studying the half-inch-long flattened leaves, arranged in two ranks on either side of the twigs—greens-on-a-stick. The leaves are a glossy green on their upper surfaces and have a pale grayish sheen beneath. If one crushes a handful of the crisp foliage, a spicy, bracing fragrance fills the air. When a man cuts hemlock trees for boards and shingles, he appreciates the beauty of the wood and the bark. The inner bark is a chestnut red. In olden days the pioneers used it for tanning leather. The wood is strikingly beautiful with its pinkish-brown tinge and streaks of deeper red and russet.

The hemlock has a steady, unpretentious beauty through all the seasons. Perhaps its greatest appeal comes in early summer —a few days after the masses of conelike, seed-bearing flowers have passed. Then there is a brief period of loveliness as the new growth shows its delicate light green in harmony with the rich, deep hue of the older leaves. In the early summer sunshine there are flashing glints of bronze, green, and brown as the rays catch the color of tiny new cones, the old foliage, and the new. The hemlock is an everyday tree, but it plays its role in bringing beauty to the countryside.

LITTLE MINNESINGER

THE cricket is a wholehearted, gregarious fellow. "Cricket on the hearth" has come to be a phrase of accepted folklore. Our Chinese friends have kept crickets as household pets since the days of long, long ago and have lavished time and affection upon them.

In the New World crickets are everyday, democratic insects inhabiting urban and rural environments impartially. They are as much a part of the summer scene as toads, hornets, and snakes. In the late afternoon when Jupiter is driving his flaming chariot downhill to the western horizon, *Gryllus* stirs from his daytime siesta and offers a tentative chirp or two prior to launching into his evening's concert.

He's a handsome chap, but there are few who have held him in hand to examine his short, rounded, greenish-black body. His leaping legs are long and slender and his feet have no pulvilli. Perhaps that is why *Gryllus* is a home-loving body and does not like to go leaping through a rough world. A jumping insect without cushions on his feet must get many jarring shocks. His bright, beady eyes are widely spaced, and his two extremely long black antennae seem constantly to probe the air ahead.

It's in the evening that *Gryllus* makes his strongest bid for recognition. On sultry nights when there's only a sliver of moon and the earth lies quietly in process of fruition, when little breeze is stirring and humanity is waiting for a turn in the weather, his concert is at its best. We do not care if he uses his wings instead of his vocal cords to produce his alto-tenor song. It's cheerful, friendly music, a bit on the monotonous side, but always optimistic and indicative of his even disposition.

OLD-FASHIONED HAMMOCK

THE countryman doesn't know all that's wrong with contemporary society. He has his own ideas about current goings on but readily admits that in a representative democracy a man is entitled to his idiosyncrasies if they do not unduly encroach upon the prerogatives of his peers. After due deliberation and comprehensive first-hand experimentation, however, he has come to the conclusion that one of the things this country needs most is a renaissance of the old-fashioned hammock that used to hang between trees in the farmstead yard.

There was something restful and relaxing about them. After a hearty dinner of fried salt pork, new boiled potatoes, and milk gravy, tamped down with a couple of pieces of blueberry pie, a man enjoyed stretching out for forty winks. An old-fashioned hammock fitted the contours of his anatomy. His head and feet were high enough for solid comfort. There was a chance for air to circulate beneath and around him. None of the cooped-up feeling engendered by high-backed, flossy swayers and gliders.

The hammocks came in satisfying and emphatic color combinations. There were deep side curtains and long wavy fringes. The ads in the mail-order catalogue told the story with wholehearted enthusiasm: "The hammock is woven as close as the finest tapestry. All the beauty and color in design of an Oriental rug. Spreader at head and foot; extra full deep curtain; fine heavy fringe; size of bed 40 by 80 inches. Upholstered and enameled button tufted throwback tassel bar. Weight 5½ pounds. Could not be duplicated elsewhere for $4. Price, $2.51."

It seems as though we are headed into a bright, glossy era of chromium and plastics, but the countryman believes that the old knitted and woven hammocks of yesteryear performed a valuable service in helping to maintain society's equilibrium.

SPRINGHOUSE

THERE was a time before science brought milking machines, electric coolers, and other mechanical marvels to the farm when the springhouse was an essential part of rural living. While it is doubtless true, as men of judgment assert, that refrigeration is one of the pivotal inventions of history, many men and women who now casually flip the handle of a mechanical cooling box can recall the days when the old springhouse served its purpose well.

Usually it was built over a stream of cold running water—a brook fed by springs that bubbled up from underground. Sometimes the house—stone, brick, or wood—was constructed directly over a never-failing spring, and the overflow went to the barnyard trough where cattle and neat stock, horses and colts, drank from the oak-planked, weather-stained, moss-lined box.

The interior of the springhouse was damp and cool. On hot days in July and August when a lad had a few minutes between loads of hay or grain, it was refreshing to slip into the moist dimness and rest and to drink a dipperful of cold, tangy buttermilk. In the walled spring area or in the running brook stood the tall cans of milk—cans with the spigots at the bottoms so that the skim milk could be drawn off for the pigs and calves. Or perhaps round tin pans of milk covered with layers of thick cream rested on rocks or bricks in the water, waiting to be skimmed with the old-fashioned hand skimmer that resembled a wide-spreading sea shell. Here were stored the pound prints of butter, each wrapped in its crinkly paper, ready to be taken to the general store to exchange for groceries.

There are still springhouses serving the needs of farm families, but year by year the number grows fewer. The small, homey structures with their cool, damp interiors have played their part in the history of a developing nation.

HAYING

A SWEET, pungent fragrance hovers over the countryside in July as freshly cut grass wilts in the hot sunshine. The staccato, monotone song of the mowing machine echoes over the meadows and floats down from the upland fields. It is haying time, and the countryman hurries to get the important crop under cover and into the big stacks by the end of the barn.

It is true that the hay harvest is a period of hustle and anxiety. The best hay comes from grasses and clovers cut at exactly the right time. There's always apprehension about what the Weather Man will send when a farmer has several tons of his best grass down. But in spite of the tension many countrymen say that they like haying the best of all the seasonal tasks in the farm schedule. Naturally, a young man of a dozen years or so claims the right to make certain mental reservations. No one can convince him that raking up the scatterings as a load is pitched on the wagon is a fellow's idea of a good time. Worst of all is the storing away on the barn scaffold. On a hot day the temperature is well over a hundred degrees under the eaves, and the man pitching off the load tosses up great forkfuls with overwhelming speed. The perspiration runs down a chap's face and back. The ticklish, prickly hayseed gets into his hair and inside his socks. But it's all a part of haying.

The work in the open field is not so bad. Sometimes a welcome, cooling breeze springs up, and along toward the end of the afternoon when the last load is finally on, the countryman who remembers the haying days of his own youth is likely to say, "Well, Son, we'll wait until morning to unload. You go get your swim and then bring home the cows." That's when the miracle occurs. A lad who was totally exhausted a few minutes earlier suddenly finds his strength completely returned as he dashes across the meadow to the swimming hole in the creek.

THE countryman tries to be patient and tolerant of the foibles of mankind. He believes it is a fundamental tenet of democracy that a man should be allowed his idiosyncrasies and peculiarities as long as they do not cause undue friction with his fellow men. From early spring until hard frost time artists depict his stone walls, pasture hillsides, and buildings. The countryman is glad to cooperate in these aesthetic ventures in oil and water color; he is mildly interested in the futuristic school of impressionism—especially since Cousin Mabel took lessons from that professor. Her modernistic rendition of the silo and icehouse is as intricate as a difficult picture puzzle.

But when he hears that the red barns of the countryside were painted such a color because his forbears had a subconscious yearning to enliven their barren lives and the drab environment of the hills and valleys, he believes the time has come for straight talking. Red cow barns, red horse barns, and red houses were painted that rich, satisfying, and lasting color because Nature provided red ocher somewhere in the neighborhood.

It was both economical and efficient for Grandfather to dig some of the red hematite iron ore, bake it in the oven, mix it with linseed oil to penetrate the wood, and add skim milk to serve as a spreader. It made a paint that would last for years. The countryman is glad that the soft, weathered red fits so well into the environment. He isn't averse to the need for aesthetics, though he has always believed that the mountains and meadows and upland fields, the sunrises and sunsets and cycling seasons gave him a satisfaction that some city folks did not appreciate. He simply wants the record straight. He's glad that the local area provided red ocher instead of purple or a pastel magenta.

WEATHER PROGNOSTICATOR

ON a sultry summer evening when the humid air lingers over the countryside and the chimney swifts are twittering in their dark homes, the tree toads begin their alto chants. There are varying degrees of intensity to their cheerful trilling. If the night is seasonably cool and the weather cycle is just starting its regular round of cumulus, cirrus, stratus, and nimbus cloud changes, *Hyla versicolor* blends his monotone theme into the night chorus. But if the humidity is high and there's likelihood of rain, the tree toad increases its volume. Then the steady, insistent, loud notes take precedence over katydids and crickets. Countrymen sitting on farm porches prophesy, "There'll be rain before morning."

Tree toads are really frogs. They are friendly little fellows but difficult to locate on trees, shrubs, stone walls, and rail fences because of their protective coloring. They change hues to match the environment. Generally ash-gray, the calm little prognosticators have streaks of green and brown blending with their main color. They have a certain jaunty grotesqueness. There's a yellowish spot below each large brilliant eye and a black oblique band above. The insides of their hind legs are bright orange, and often an irregular star-shaped design appears on their backs. They have four large fingers and five

60

long toes, each finger and toe equipped with an adhesive disk.

Hyla reminds one of a miniature fantastic beast that may have roamed the land long ago when fern trees grew in steamy jungles. In the warm darkness of a summer evening it's pleasant to sit and listen to his optimistic notes. He plays a steady tune while the fireflies put on their lantern ballet.

STRAWBERRY SOCIAL

THE village organizations that put on an annual strawberry social have a time-tested formula that insures financial success. The townsfolk and farmers donate the berries, cream, sugar, sandwiches, and cake. Then they come to the social and pay a fair price for their own goods. The countryman does not pretend to be an economic expert. He does fairly well in a horse trade and is never averse to the purchase of a likely milker. But, as he mildly remarks after buying a dish or two of his own big, red berries, the ladies of the Grange or the sewing circle ought to be running the finances of the government. Naturally, as he goes on to explain, he would dislike to be on the lease end of a lend-lease affair if the ladies were out to raise money to shingle the White House instead of the Grange Hall.

A strawberry social is different from a baked-bean supper or a dinner of the historical society. It is outdoors, for one thing, and there is a holiday-picnic atmosphere about it. The ladies like it because it is comparatively simple to put on and the profit is always large. Almost everyone is willing to buy two dishes of berries, and at ten cents a dish, plus a nickel for each sandwich and each piece of cake, there is money to be made. A man who has been hoeing corn or potatoes all day has a healthy appetite, and he is perfectly willing to buy several sandwiches—provided they are his wife's. He does not want any of those fancy little affairs with a bit of chopped lettuce and parsley between two wafer-thin slices of bread.

The food, however, is only one attraction of the strawberry social. It gives people a chance to visit and get caught up on the news. The menfolks get together and talk about the solid subjects that men everywhere need to discuss—weather, crops, livestock, and politics. The womenfolks exchange recipes, patterns, and the problems of their respective households. A strawberry social is a traditional part of American life—a chance for human beings to display good fellowship and neighborliness.

OLD SWIMMIN' HOLE

THE old swimmin' hole is one of the links that help to hold together the regions of a great nation. It's all to the good in towns and cities for society to build cement-lined pools with chemically treated water where youngsters can have fun, but such pools are far different propositions from a swimming hole in creek or brook. Hidden by willows and alders, a country swimming hole is strictly a masculine sanctuary where young men can swim and dive and splash without encumbering raiment.

A first-class swimming hole has a number of essential accessories in addition to its seclusion from the general public.

It must have a deep spot where a long, overhanging, springy plank gives a fellow a chance for a high flip as he starts his dive. It ought to have a sandbar where he can loll between periods of activity. And interest is added if there's an overhanging bank where turtles and water snakes retreat when humankind invades their realm.

The countryman who remembers the days of his youth looks with understanding eyes at lads who are utterly exhausted from their labors along about four o'clock of a summer's afternoon. It is hot, dusty, itchy work to stow the hay away under the eaves of the barn. It is monotonous, drudging labor for a fourteen-year-older to pull the bull rake and gather up the scatterings. Or perhaps a fellow has been following the cultivator behind a faithful horse—back and forth, back and forth, between the rows of corn. A miracle occurs when Father says, "Well, boys, I guess we'll call it a day. You get your swim and then bring home the cows." Strength suddenly returns to youthful muscles. Life becomes worth living. There's a race to the creek, a flinging aside of overalls, shirt, shoes, and socks. Few pleasures are keener than that first plunge into cold water on a hot midsummer's day.

BAND CONCERT

MANY men and women now living and working in cities remember the band concerts that were an expected part of the summer social season in the country. Every Wednesday evening during July and August the Centerville Town Band climbed into the circular bandstand on the village common and gave a concert. For ten months its members had been working and rehearsing. In their blue coats with the yellow braid and big yellow buttons, freshly pressed white duck trousers, and snappy visored caps that reminded one of high naval officers' headgear, they presented an imposing appearance. It was hard to realize that the handsome, dignified man blowing the tuba was Jeff Smith who ran the grain mill, or that the tall, distinguished-looking conductor was Eben Jones who published the local weekly. Soft, golden light from the kerosene lamps with big reflectors made a beautiful contrast with the darkness outside. Not that the men needed light; they knew the pieces by heart.

Farm families came from miles around—whole families in two-seated democrats; elderly couples in fringed-top surreys; young folks who sat holding hands in stylish top buggies. Sometimes the teams were put in the horse sheds behind the church and the town hall, and the people sat on blankets around the common. "Not too close," Father used to say. "Music is better at a little distance." However, young men of eight or ten summers believed that the nearer they got, the better the concert. The applause was generous, and Eben always gave his famous bow, an imitation of the bow he had seen at a big concert in the city.

It did not matter that the audience also knew the pieces by heart. The music the band played was the kind that could bear repetition—stirring marches, waltzes, and the folk songs that will live forever: "Annie Laurie," "Swanee River," "Flow Gently, Sweet Afton," and "Old Black Joe." And when at last it grew late (a little after nine), the band always played "Good Night, Ladies." It was the custom for everyone to sing with them. Out through the peaceful night floated the sweet music, slow in tempo, but gloriously melodious, as several hundred men and women, boys and girls joined in. The band concerts may not have been great music, but they were music from the heart.

WAITING DAYS

AUGUST drags out its days on sticky, muffled feet. The sun re-
luctantly pulls itself above the horizon's rim and starts its
course across a washed, blue sky. Rag-puff mists blossom
briefly on the lowlands. Twice in each cycle of the months
there is a period of quietness. Each hushed period precedes a
time of activity. February and August are times of muted music.

Now waters creep quietly on their way to the sea, and tall
elms in the meadows stand motionless through humid hours.
Golden pollen drifts from the corn tassels to the green skeins
of drooping silk beneath. Goldenrod raises its banners beside
stone walls, and wild asters make patches of blue in field corners. Sumac pennants are changing from russet brown to wine
red. On pasture hillsides stiff-stemmed hardhack lifts timothy-
like spires to the hot sun.

Quietness rests thickly on the countryside. Occasionally a
song sparrow takes his stance on the garden gate and tosses an
aria to an indifferent world. From the sugar bush high on the
hillside come the intermittent, querulous caws of young crows.
Big bumblebees drone phlegmatically from flower to flower
and ruby-throated hummingbirds hover before the second-
blooming delphiniums.

Dusk tiptoes hesitatingly down from the hills after scarlet
sunsets. Night's curtain is drawn on smoothly running pulleys.
Chimney swifts twitter softly in their nests, and nighthawks'
thin hollow booms rise from the oat stubble. Tree toads blow

their monotone clarinets, and crickets bow their alto notes. Fireflies draw red dashes on night's dark page. These are waiting days—waiting for the first cool scouts of autumn to foretell a new season.

TIN PEDDLER

THE annual visit of the tin peddler to the farm was an event of great importance. On an August afternoon a farm lad would spot him coming far down the road. As he turned into the yard, the whole family would be waiting to greet him. His call was much more than an impersonal commercial matter. The tin peddler of yesteryear was a friend. He had known the family for a generation; he brought news from relatives and acquaintances that one saw only once a year at the county fair.

His large boxlike cart was always fascinating. On the outside hung all kinds of pails, brooms, shovels, cooking utensils, baskets, coils of rope, and strips of leather. Inside, there were boxes of all shapes and sizes holding scores of things needed by the farm housewife—needles and pins, china and cutlery. One section was filled with bolts of cloth—gaily patterned ginghams and percales and packages of beautiful satins and silks. There was material for window curtains and rolls of laces. When he spread his material on the big kitchen table, it was more exciting than the arrival of the purchases from the mail-order company.

The tin peddler bought as well as sold. He was always eager to get rags of linen and good wool, and Mother usually had a bagful for him. Oftentimes he would spend the night, and in the evening neighbors would come in to hear him tell wonderful stories of his boyhood days in far-off Armenia. And when he left in the morning, he always handed a bag of wonderful hard candies to each youngster and a colorful vase or a bit of exquisite lace to Mother.

The tin peddlers brought color and brightness to farm homes on lonesome country roads. Although they have almost disappeared, many a man and woman now living in the city can remember the thrill of that youthful day in late summer when the shout went up, "The peddler's coming!"

QUIET BROOKS

IN the period of midsummer quietness after the urgency of spring has spent its force, the hush of August broods over the countryside. The time of fulfillment approaches, and Earth waits in patient expectancy. At dawn there are only a few bird calls; the poignant sweet song of the hermit thrush comes at dusk. And the brooks run quietly to join the rivers.

A few weeks ago the brooks ran full between their banks and sang gayly as they welcomed a new season. Now the wheel of time has turned a quarter cycle on its rim, and the waters move languidly and softly over the pebbles and exposed roots. Back on the hillsides and in mountain ravines small streams start the journey to the sea. Trickles of water flow down the slopes; they join other rivulets and form small brooks.

Through shadowed ravines, beneath plank bridges, and through the woodlands twist the moving waters. Under grass banks speckled trout face upstream during the quiet days. The

little brooks join larger brooks and creeks in the meadow lowlands and add their volume to the descending waters. Tall
willows and stocky alder clumps shade the larger brooks.
Muskrats poke along the exposed mud banks, and deer cross
the meadows at dawn. Kingfishers sit on limbs; bitterns send
their hollow thumpings from the swampy spots. Always the
brooks run quietly. Earth's pulse is calm and unhurried in
August, and the moving waters match the mood of the season.

RASPBERRY GLADES

FOLLOW an old rutted road bordered with hardhack across the
sloping shoulder of an upland pasture. Go through the sugar
bush where the massive, rough-barked maples stand steadfast
through the seasons. Twist and turn with the road as it winds
through spruces and hemlocks around the brow of the hill.
Deep in the woods where an area of evergreens was cut off two
or three winters ago you will find the raspberry glades.

Wild raspberries are different from their domesticated cousins. The fire-red juicy berries have a tangy goodness that reminds one of cool moist dawns, spring rains, and woodland
shadows. In a deep-dish pie or fluffy cobbler they give a flavor
that cannot be matched by the fruit of the cultivated brambles.

Wild raspberries are part of Nature's healing touch. When
an area is first cut over, stark gashed stumps and brown-black
limb slash make a desolate scene. By midsummer, if the soil is
deep and fertile, the ground is green with ferns, sweet wild
grasses, and the slender stalks of raspberries. The first-year
canes are greenish-gold willowy stems; the leaves are a light

70

gray-green hue. By the second season the stumps and slash are hidden, and the biennial bramble offers generous yield of its fruits.

Stand at the edge of a raspberry glade early in the morning, and the woodland picture has the misty beauty of a Corot. The slanting rays of light reflect many shades of green; the red berries hang like jewels from the bent canes. Two or three times a season the countryman likes to take a five-quart lard pail and go for wild raspberries. The fruit is the tangible motive, but the peaceful solitude and beauty the glade offers are an intangible reward.

FRIED SALT PORK

FRIED salt pork is more or less out of fashion now except for a few discerning countrymen who know its inherent tangy goodness. In an era of food metamorphosis when edibles come frozen, dehydrated, concentrated, and precooked, fried salt pork is likely to be dismissed without due consideration. In late August when a man has had his fill of fried chicken, chicken pie, and chicken fricassee, he sort of hankers for a meal of the salty, crunchy meat.

There's a natural affinity between the pork and the rest of the meal. Patient experimentation has proved that boiled potatoes and milk gravy are the fate-blessed concomitants of the crisp, saliva-starting slices. Since last winter the chunks of pork have been floating in the dark crackly brine in the wooden barrel beneath the cellar stairs. A good husbandman likes to know that there is plenty of the meat for his Saturday night baked beans and as the foundation for his fish chowder.

There are a few basic essentials one must observe in preparing the dish. The pork must have strips of lean in it to furnish satisfying, long-lasting chewing. The slices must be freshened a few hours in tepid water. Keep the pot on the third cover of the stove from 7:30 A.M. to 11:30 A.M. Slice it exactly five-sixteenths of an inch thick, roll it in flour, and fry it slowly in an iron spider over an ash and oak fire. Take off the stove cover the last few minutes so the hot meat will make a crisp outer covering. A half-dozen slices of the fragrant, tart-crusted salt pork, with new potatoes and rich milk gravy, plus a few biscuits with currant jelly, two slices of juicy, deep-dish apple pie, and a glass or two of cold creamy milk comprise a satisfying dinner in the countryman's estimation.

LITTLE OPTIMIST

THE farmyard wouldn't seem natural without a pair of the little fellows. Whether the skies are blue or gray, they perch on the icehouse, woodshed, or barnyard gate and pour forth their rollicking song. The pert, bold house wrens with their up-turned tails are birds with personality. They are thoroughgoing extroverts. They enjoy the bustle of human activity about the farm buildings and seem to feel it their duty to greet the countryman whenever he crosses the yard.

Troglodytes aedon is a handsome, stylish chap. His back is a soft cinnamon brown; his stubby, upraised tail is crossbarred with streaks of black. His wings are peculiarly long for such a miniature troubadour and are jauntily streaked with dark bars. His waistcoat is a soft smoke gray. Sometimes as he sits on the barnyard gate and accosts the farmer on his way to do the

73

morning milking, it seems as though he enjoys showing off a bit. He sings his rippling song with utmost abandon and all the time keeps his bright eyes on the man. He likes to lean far forward as he sings and he flips his perky tail as if to punctuate the fortissimo movements in his aria.

He and his demure mate build their nests in a somewhat haphazard fashion, stuffing twigs and coarse grasses into a hole or crevice in a tree or a nook in a building. The loose-looking home, however, is well lined with soft grass. The tiny eggs are pink buff or pinkish brown in color with specks of deeper brown and a brown wreath around the larger ends.

On late summer days when a man comes in from cutting brush along the stone walls, it's good to be welcomed by the wren. He flies to the woodshed roof and bubbles over with his loud, clear, happy song. Other birds are quiet in the waning season. Not so *Troglodytes.* Until he leaves for his winter home along the Gulf Coast, he sees that there is music around the farmyard.

LICKING THE DASHER

MODERN progress is all very well with its scientific gadgets, horseless carriages, airplanes, and bubble gum of balloon proportions. The countryman does not oppose mechanical refrigerators where one can flip a switch and produce ice cream without turning the crank of a freezer. He does regret, however, that more lads of a dozen years or so cannot enjoy the superlative satisfaction of licking the dasher.

On a hot, sultry August afternoon when the perspiration trickled down the forehead and made a rivulet down the middle of one's back, Father would sometimes say, "Son, why don't you see if Mother will make us some ice cream for supper? You help her and I'll finish up this job." A lad's flagging strength was quickly renewed. It wasn't hard work to get a big chunk of green-white ice from the sawdust in the weathered icehouse. No work at all to pound the pieces fine in a meal bag. Turning the crank of the six-quart freezer could not be compared with the drudgery of turning the heavy grindstone.

Round and round in the ice and salt went the metal cylindrical can. Salt water ran out the hole near the bottom of the wooden freezer. By and by, the mixture of eggs, sugar, cream, and flavoring began to harden. Funny how Father always managed to appear just as the last hard turning finished. He would give a few tentative turns and pronounce the verdict, "I guess she's done." The ice and salt were taken from the top; the cover was removed.

The rest of the family had small saucerfuls as preliminary tastes, but a boy had the dasher in a dishpan. An understanding Mother always left plenty of the cold, creamy deliciousness on the wooden paddles. A fellow could sit down on the chopping block and slowly, appreciatively savor the satisfying goodness. Many men can look back on their youth and remember the days of long ago when they helped make ice cream—and had the dasher to lick as a reward.

THE WEAVERS

SUMMER is the season of the milkweed. The stately plants with their beautiful purple-red, flat-topped buds and creamy-white blossoms tinged with pink grow along the country roadsides, in the fence corners, and beside the stone walls. Patches of them stand like sentinels behind the barns and the icehouses. In the back yard they spring up around the spot where the wood was piled.

The milkweed is attractive from the time it pushes through the soil until the last seed has unraveled from its skein of woven silk and floated away. As it comes through the ground in May, each soft white leaf is wrapped lengthwise around the stem. As the plant grows, the handsome, sturdy leaves develop in pairs. When fully mature each leaf is a thing of beauty. The central vein is a deep reddish purple; the alternate side veins are greenish white with tiny, irregular veins forming an uneven pattern of faint lines.

It's the weaving of the silk for which the milkweed is most famous. The milkweed pod provides tenacious protection while Nature's shuttle and loom are performing the mystery of maturing. On a day in August the pod with its finished selvage-seam edges begins to open, and inside one can see the skein of lustrous, tightly wrapped white silk with the light-rimmed, brown, overlapped seeds. Then the glossy silk begins to separate into airy floss. Each seed has its own balloon of shiny, fluffy threads; in these white parachutes they float away.

The milkweed is not a favorite flower of the countryman. There are too many of them; the weavers send their seeds far and wide. But as a man comes across his fields in August and sees the clumps of striking blossoms filling in the hedgerows along the fences, he isn't too concerned. Milkweed gives a touch of welcome color to the countryside after the fields and meadows have been shorn of their first crops.

76

COVERED bridges are gradually disappearing. The few that still remain are memorials to yesteryear when life was more leisurely and flavorful. Today there's a staccato roar as hurrying cars shoot through the weathered, picturesque old structures that span rivers and creeks. Only a bit more than a generation ago there was a rhythmic, hollow echoing as horses thumped their hoofs on the gray splintery wood and iron-rimmed wheels rolled over the wide planks.

Covered bridges were built to serve a utilitarian need, but no one has completely settled the question as to whether bridges were covered to protect the framework or whether farmers believed their horses would be frightened to cross a long open bridge. A century ago certain bridge builders were identified by the different arches that they devised.

A young man of a dozen years liked a covered bridge. It was fun to crawl across the timbers beneath the roof. If the bridge had an open latticework side, he could work his way slowly across above the water. There was no point in going through a bridge if one could go along the outside. A fellow was expected to take a reasonable amount of time getting home from district school. Beneath the bridge it was cool and moist. The abutment rocks were green and slippery with close-growing moss. There was always the chance he would see the famous big trout that disdained worms and grasshoppers. Sometimes there was a large snapping turtle. Often a long water snake would go slithering by. When a double team passed through the bridge, the reverberating roar was like a long roll of thunder.

The old covered bridges are part of our country's heritage. They stand patiently through the seasons. Growing fewer year by year, they remind us of the painstaking craftsmen of long ago who helped build a nation which is still climbing to its destined stature.

BLACKBERRYING

THERE comes a day in August when the countryman likes to take a five-quart lard pail and go blackberrying. It's an in-between time on the farm, and a man has a pleasant sense of leisure as he waits for the fall harvest season. The berries are plump and juicy and hang heavily on the canes in the southeast corner of the upland pasture.

One rarely wishes to dispute with Mr. Webster, but when he merely states that blackberries are a bramble of the rose family with black fruit, one feels that less than justice has been done. In the first place, if the season has been generous with moisture and heat, the big, shiny berries hanging thickly on the vines are an attractive sight. Wild raspberries are modest and retiring; they like the seclusion of nooks and glades. Blackberries, however, are extroverts; they want to be seen. They hold their handsome berries up to the sun.

In the second place, something should be said about the blackberry vines. One doesn't wade carelessly into the tangled jungle of tough, prickly canes. The vines are tall and strong; they are covered with needle-pointed spines that command respect. But in spite of the spines it's satisfying work. If the countryman fastens the pail by a suspender loop, he can use both hands until the weight grows too heavy. In a good spot he can pick for several minutes at a time.

On a sunny, not-too-hot day when a man can stop occasionally to look at the old sugar grove above him and take time to study the blues and greens on the mountain across the valley, it's a pleasant task to fill the pail with the dead-ripe, sweetly tart berries. And in the evening when he comes in from milking, he knows that after the fried potatoes and corn bread there'll be a big dish of blackberry cobbler covered with plenty of rich yellow cream. To be sure, there are hazards connected with blackberrying, but the reward is in keeping.

CROQUET

WHAT this country needs most may be a matter that won't be settled for a considerable period. There can be little doubt in the countryman's mind, however, that a nationwide revival of the blood-tingling, ask-and-give-no-quarter game of lawn croquet would help get the nation back on an even keel.

At the turn of the century, a man had a reserve of strength and nervous energy left at the end of a day's living. He looked forward to a few games of croquet in the evening as a prelude to the porch-sitting hour. One can imagine that the golf and tennis addicts, the mountain hikers and cross-country bicyclists, feel a pitying disdain for a man who enjoys knocking wooden balls through little wickets. Croquet is different, of course, from these outdoor pursuits. It is much less strenuous and requires a much smaller financial investment. But there are other less tangible reasons why the countryman of today feels that croquet is needed in our contemporary civilization.

It's an unhurried game. A man has to keep calm and serene. He has to do some nice calculating as to the best way of dispersing his opponents' balls or of using them to further his progress around the route. When he misses an easy shot, there's the need for nonchalance, the cultivation of a "what's the difference" attitude. The comments—caustic, jibing, flattering, and derogatory—must be taken in his stride. The game develops muscular control and keen judgment. It affords a surprising amount of pleasant exercise. We countrymen wouldn't turn the clock of progress back; no doubt there are reasons for the screaming thousands at the ball parks, the multitudes at the prize fights, and the throngs at the race courses. We merely ask in a mild sort of way if there isn't some method of restoring a game that offers pleasurable recreation on a modest scale.

MIST OVER MEADOWS

THERE is beauty on the meadows in the cool, moist mornings. Through humid days the brassy sun circles near the pole of the horizon. A heat blanket lies over the shorn hayfields. Bird music is muted and water courses quietly in pebbly-bottomed brooks. Corn leaves curl their edges, and clumps of white birches on boulder-dotted upland pastures stand patiently above the brown, sun-cured grasses.

When the first fingers of soft-colored light show above the meeting line of earth and sky, the meadows are gray-white ponds. The deep blanket of mist conceals the willows along the creek and hides the tall vaselike elms that dot the mowing. The land patiently waits for the sun to pull in night's cover.

When the sun lifts above the horizon and the slanting rays pierce the mist, there is an interlude of loveliness. Minute by minute the mist grows thinner. The shadowy shapes of the trees show dimly through the mistiness. In a few minutes one can see the dark, winding outline of the waterway. As the main body of mist disappears, small ponds of the whiteness linger at low spots like white blossoms carelessly tossed on the gold-green floor of the meadow.

At dawn there is welcome coolness in the air. Soon the sun will throw its heat over the countryside. But for a time there is beauty on the meadows in the mornings.

BEAUTIFUL MONTH

THERE'S something about September that sets it apart from other months. There are days of mellow heat when a soft blue haze hovers over the fields and brows of hills; there are crisp, starlit nights when chill breezes sweep through meadow mowings and upland pastures. It's an off season on the farm, and the quiet brooding spirit of the period gives a welcome sense of leisureliness after the summer's rush of growth and harvest.

Chipmunks scamper along the rail fences, building up caches of food against the time of cold. Crows begin to gather for their fall conventions and settle in flocks in the stubble of the fields. The songbirds gather in clans and swoop over the gardens and meadows. Along country roads sumacs hold their scarlet banners aloft, and in fence corners wild blue asters lift their beauty to the sun. In the swamps, the stiff spikes of cattails are changing their deep brown cylindrical heads to the light brown they will wear through the winter. Here and there among the swamp maples in the marshes and among the scrub oaks on thin-soiled upland hillsides a flaming bouquet of red leaves tells its tale of a season's passing.

It's a time of quiet waiting. Gone now is the hurry of summer and the impatience of developing maturity. Mornings are cool and the atmosphere warms slowly. In the afternoons, the shadows begin to creep across the fields as the countryman goes to his chores. There's no longer the drawn-out interlude between dusk and darkness. Toward the end of day, gray banners of smoke spiral upward from farm chimneys and drift away

83

to nothingness. Lights begin to appear in kitchens. As a man comes in with the milk pails over his arm and anticipates the chill of approaching night, he has a sense of contentment. September is a beautiful month—and doubly so when a golden shaft of light from a kitchen window makes a path for a man's feet.

BRACKEN

GO to the hardwood ridges on a late summer day and watch the sun's rays paint a picture of mullioned beauty on the three-branched ferns. Bracken is a sturdy, individualistic plant with tall, coarse stems. In the mingled sunlight and shadow one can see a dozen shades of green blending together in an appealing picture.

Bracken does not have the fragile beauty and laciness of the toothed woodfern or the delicate symmetry of the hay-scented fern. *Pteridium latiusculum* has no airs or pretensions. While most of the fern family prefer damp, dim spots, bracken takes thin upland soil for its home. One will also find it in spreading clumps on boulder-studded upland pastures and on the sandy sides of ravines. On rocky banks above pasture swamps it fills in the open spaces among the gray birches. In old sidehill sugar orchards one often sees extensive patches of the three-foot-tall ferns growing around the big rough-barked maple trees. Occasionally there is a necklace of bracken circling the outside edge of a grove of spruces and hemlocks.

When summer draws on, the faint dots or spore cases make

a line along the pinnules. Soon the spores will ripen and split open, and the minute particles will be scattered by the wind. Unlike most seeds, the germination of a spore does not mean an immediate new plant. The spore grows into a small organism of evanescent tissue. From this tissue comes the prothallium, a Greek word meaning "before the shoot." The prothallium produces organs corresponding to stamens and pistils of flowers; after fertilization a fern plant is born. Seven years are needed for a fern to reach mature growth from a spore.

September is a good time to see the bracken. Its widespreading tops make a pattern in the sun. It is one of the humble plants that help give cover to the land.

FIRST SCHOOL DAY

MR. SHAKESPEARE was only partially correct in his famous description of a very young man on his way to school. All schoolboys do not go unwillingly when it's time for teacher to ring the bell for the first day of a new term. Most boys and girls in spite of some expected talk to the contrary look forward to the organized routine of working and playing together.

The little one-room building at the crossroads is one of the bulwarks of a great nation. Each summer it is cleaned and it may be given a new coat of paint. Perhaps there will be a new blackboard. Cords of good solid oak, ash, and hickory are stored away to keep the big, round stove hot during the cold months. The school is humble and unpretentious inside, with its old battered desks (the teacher's on a low platform), its rows of hooks in the entry for coats and hats, and the shelf where farm boys and girls place their lunch boxes until the hands of the old clock point to twelve.

Teacher has to handle all eight grades, but she knows the strengths and weaknesses of each boy and girl as teachers in big city schools never get to know their children. Older pupils help the younger ones. Big boys know that if they master their lessons, they will have a chance to keep the water pail filled and to tend the fire in the stove. Strange how much time a young man can use in attending to these tasks. Many a father and mother who have trouble in keeping the wood box behind the kitchen stove filled are mildly surprised to hear that Johnny is such a good fireman at school.

It is time for school bells to ring again. Along the country roads boys and girls are responding to them willingly. When teacher steps to the doorway and swings the bell that means it is time to line up, it also means that democracy is in action. First day of school is a rich tradition in the history of a great nation.

BEE LINING

WHEN the first frost has deepened the bloom on juniper berries and the last page of summer's book has slowly closed, the countryman takes a day off and lines himself a bee tree. For the benefit of the uninitiated it should be explained that each year swarms of domesticated bees leave their hives behind barns and woodsheds and seek homes in trees in the woods. A newly hatched queen carries on the housekeeping in the hive; the old queen and some thousands of her retinue go to the frontier spot discovered by the advance scouts.

Bee lining is neither mysterious nor complicated. A man takes a section of comb honey in a small covered box to an open field where asters and goldenrod hold their blossoms to the sky. A bee comes to the box. After he has loaded, he takes off in a straight line for his tree home. As he returns with friends, one notes the direction. When the next group comes back, the cover is put on the box. A man walks as far as he thinks wise in the direction the bees flew; then he releases the bees. After half a dozen or perhaps a dozen such stops and starts, he comes to the tree. Half way up the trunk there is likely to be a knot hole through which the bees are coming and going. That's the mechanical part of bee lining.

It's interesting to know that it takes approximately a hundred thousand bee miles to gather a pound of nectar. But a man enjoys bee lining for other than the material gains which are his when the tree is felled. It is good to be out in the fields and woods. There's a heart lift in the blue sky overhead and in the purple haze on distant mountains. Crickets rasp their fiddles and grasshoppers take off on short whirring flights. Over the land is the warm, calm beauty of September. Bee lining has a long history and much folklore tradition; it also has intangibles that are more important than pailfuls of honey.

THERE'S something about a rail fence that fits the environment. A long, long time ago man made the discovery that fences served his needs, a discovery that ranks with that of domesticating grains to insure his food or evolving the free-turning wheel to help bear his burdens. Fences are guardians of crops and protectors of boundaries.

Made of the materials at hand, the weather-grayed, homey-type structure rambles along in zigzag fashion by the sides of meandering country roads. It climbs in a sort of leisurely, casual way over the slopes of fields and along pasture hillsides. It dips and circles and rises to fit the contour of the land which grew the wood of which it is made.

One of two chief kinds of rail fences is the zigzag type, with the interlocking ends of rails, that goes back and forth even as it goes ahead. This gives the angle necessary for the large-sized rails to rest on each other. The other type is the post-and-rail affair, where the posts are set in line and have holes into which the smaller-sized rails are fitted. Each type is indigenous to the landscape; each serves many purposes besides the self-evident one of acting as a boundary.

Along the tops squirrels scamper as they hustle in their winter stores. Over the fences along roads and between pasture and mowing fields, alders and birches and dogwood bend. Beneath them the woodchuck likes to dig his den to be near the clover patch and the farm garden. Through gaps in old fences where rails have tumbled to the ground, the foxes and deer make their trails as they travel on their daily rounds.

Rail fences are the cross-stitching on the patchwork quilt of

the landscape. They are a memorial to the craftsmanship of men of other years who built well with the materials then available. Wire may be more efficient, but rail fences suit the heart.

THISTLEBIRD

THERE'S nothing moody or unpredictable about the goldfinch. When September's mellowness blesses the countryside and the fields, pastures, and meadows are blankets of sun-cured brown grasses, flocks of the wild canaries swirl over the landscape in distinctive undulating flight. The ladies are demurely outfitted in subdued gray-green hues, but the males are jaunty, handsome fellows in bright gold cloaks. Their wings and tails are glossy black with white bars; they wear a black cap at a rakish angle on their forehead.

The folklore name, thistlebird, comes from the goldfinch's predilection for the prickly weed. The soft down of the blossom furnishes lining for his nest; the ripe seeds are a favorite part of his menu. They are happy, gregarious birds. During the spring and early summer they delay nest building until weed seeds are ripe and the down of the thistles is ready. One often sees young fledglings in September when more forehanded birds have concluded the season's housekeeping and family duties.

Second only to the bobolinks' music is the rollicking, gay-hearted singing of the goldfinches. Their scintillating arias are heard late into fall. When other birds are quiet as they gather for the southward trip, the thistlebirds continue to spray music over the fields. It is incongruous that such carefree happy-hearted birds should be labeled with a ponderous scientific name, *Spinus tristis tristis*. But what's in a name? As the birds run through their repertory of cheerful songs while circling over garden and field or gathering in weed patches for feeding, they show that a man-given identification tag is no deterrent to their spirits.

PICKING APPLES

WHEN summer has turned the corner into fall, when mornings are bright and crisp and evenings have an edge of chill, it is time for the farmer to get his equipment together to pick apples. The countryman is particular about the job. The first fall apples are not so important, though he is as partial as any member of the family to the first apple pies and applesauce, but when it comes to the Baldwins, the Greenings, the Russets, and the Northern Spies, it is a touchy proposition. These varieties, that mean good food and good eating far into next spring, must be picked at exactly the right moment. If allowed to hang on the trees too long, they get overripe and do not keep well. If picked too early, they do not develop their full, rich flavors.

Picking apples is satisfying work. It is not a job a man can rush. It requires care to set the tall ladder so it will be firm. Then a man harvests the fruit as he works his way up through the tree. The big plump apples come off easily if one gives just the right twist of the wrist. The half-bushel basket with its wooden hook hangs from a rung of the ladder. Clinging with one hand to the ladder, a man can reach far to either side. When the picking is good, the basket fills quickly and the full boxes on the ground multiply rapidly. By the middle of the afternoon it is time to hitch old Jerry to the farm wagon and pull the loads to the cool, earth-floored cellar.

Although picking apples is work, it is work the countryman enjoys. On a sunny September day a man likes to pause a moment to look over the land from his vantage point high on the ladder. There is a brooding spirit of season's end over the meadows, fields, and upland pastures. Crickets chirp in the grass and pheasants call from the woods' edge. Fall is the beautiful interlude between summer and winter, and apple picking is one of the enjoyable tasks before the King of the Northland sends his legions of snow and cold.

COUNTY FAIR

GOING to the fair was an exciting expedition. Mother and the girls packed big lunch hampers with roasted chickens, bread, cakes, cookies, and pickles. Father hitched the Morgans to the two-seated democrat. On the morning of the big day the family was up at three o'clock, and by five everyone was ready to start. It was fun to ride behind the briskly trotting horses along the valley road, through a town or two, and over the ridge to the county seat.

The day at the fair grounds followed a pattern established by years of experience. While Father and the boys made the rounds of the long cattle sheds, saw the sheep, the hogs, and the weight-pulling contest, Mother and the girls spent their time in the handicraft building, inspecting the patchwork quilts, hooked rugs, sewing, and embroidery. At noon there was a big picnic lunch, with families and friends gathering in the grove at the end of the fair grounds. In the afternoon there were exhibits of fruits and vegetables to see and the trotting races to watch.

A twelve-year-old lad wanted to take in all these things, of course. But in addition he had to ride the merry-go-round, the ferris wheel, and the bucking donkey. He spent several dimes on games of chance and several more on big handfuls of the air-filled, flimsy spun candy. He drank too many bottles of root beer and ate too much ice cream. He marveled at the acrobats in their show on the platform before the grandstand, and made an ironclad resolution that some day he would be an acrobat and travel all over the land.

In the late afternoon the farm teams began rolling homeward. It had been a strenuous and exciting day. County fair was over for another year.

KATYDID

WHEN the blue-gold mellowness of early September blesses the land at midday and the evenings begin to whisper of autumn's coming crispness, the katydids' nightly concerts rise to fortissimo proportions. According to folklore tradition the first real frost comes six weeks after the night criers begin their singing. The countryman has a deep-rooted respect for the sayings that have evolved through the generations but he has grown skeptical of the katydids' prophesying ability.

93

The insect that makes continuous night music is a cousin to the grasshopper and the cricket. He has two long distinctive antennae; his color is a beautiful shade of light silvery green. He has tremendous wings for a small insect, but instead of flying he gives a powerful jump with his long, double-hinged hind legs and glides to his destination. He does most of his eating during daylight hours and builds up his energy for the night fiddling.

Hour after hour the monotone sounds fill the air. The left wing is scraped across the hard tough vein of the right one. There are those who assert that the staccato trilling grows monotonous, but katydid keeps calling. It is his love song and he is persistent. Soon now the music will diminuendo. The female will lay eggs in the soft bark of shrub branches. The adults will die when the first black frost blights the land. In the spring a new orchestra will start the cycle of life. For a brief period while cold legions are gathering on northern tundras, the katydids play their final song. It is at once an au revoir to summer and a hail to autumn.

COUNTRY ROADS

HARDENED arteries of cement and macadam have been stitched on today's countryside. From city to city and town to town they carry the nation's rubber-wheeled traffic. But back from the speeding streams of commerce stretch quiet, unpretentious country roads. They wind along beside singing brooks and shadowed creeks; they climb hardwood ridges and meander unhurriedly from farm to farm. They twist and curve along the contours of the land, often following the first trails established long ago by pioneers with dreams of new homes in their hearts.

The roads dip into peaceful hollows where weather-grayed, splintered plank bridges cross small streams. Around many of the humble bridges are the brook crossings where farmers drove their teams in hot weather. It was good to let the horses' brittle hoofs get wet and to have the moisture swell the dry fellies of the wheels on buckboards, democrats, and farm wagons. At the turn of the century, country roads had three tracks—two hard-packed paths where wheels rolled and a deeply scuffed horse path in the center. They were scraped in spring with log drags, and in the heart of winter big barrel-like rollers pressed down the snow.

Today one can read a part of our country's history in the semiabandoned roads. Long ago men built stone walls and zigzag split-rail fences along them. Now the fences are half hidden by bushes, trees, goldenrod, and asters. Grass crowds in from the sides; hills are gullied and thank-you-ma'ams worn flat. Cellar holes and stark chimneys are poignant reminders of the days when the quiet roads were well populated.

In September the old dirt roads drowse in mellow sunshine. They no longer fit our needs, but their peace and beauty remind us of the stirring role they once played in the drama of a nation's growth.

OCTOBER GLORY

IN autumn, stand high on an upland pasture and see glory on the land. Now is the fulfillment time of Nature's beauty. Over the hardwood ridges there's a flaming blanket of red and scarlet, brown and bronze, yellow and gold.

Sunrise is an exploding rocket of brilliant colors. White frosts rest on tanned grasses in the morning. Blue-black smoke plumes curl upward from farm chimneys and drift slowly away on the air like long hyphens. There may be thin silvery ice sheets on watering troughs and along the edges of swamp pools. The last of the summer birds gather for their long trip south. Squirrels dash along zigzag rail fences and weathered stone walls. Solitary crows stalk among the corn shocks. A shimmering purplish haze floats over meadows, mowings, and mountainsides at midday. In noonday warmth a few grasshoppers whir through the air, and phlegmatic bees explore the zinnias in the flower bed beneath the kitchen window.

Loveliness and peace rest on the countryside as farmers go about fall tasks. In the woodland the sun's slanting rays make a pattern of mullioned beauty through the colored leaves. Here and there in a meadow field or on a hillside individual trees are gorgeous flaming bouquets. Toward the end of day a chill creeps into the air. Sunsets are brief painted pictures in the sky, and then the last thin fingers of light pull night's curtain quickly over the land. Blue-green .mountains turn to purple-black, and pewter-gray shadows stride down from the heights. Stars prick through the dark veil across the sky. A

97

great yellow moon sails serenely among them. The village lights at the head of the valley make a faint halo in the distant darkness. October's peace blesses Earth.

CHUG-SUG

UNLESS he has been too active in the garden, there's an engaging quality about a woodchuck. Wejack, as the Algonquins called him, is a sort of elder statesman among the smaller animals. He sits on the doorstep of his burrow in calm, bewhiskered dignity. The fluffy gray hair on his cheeks, his widely spaced eyes and plump, well-fed figure give him the mien of a philosopher who regards the world with amused, tolerant skepticism. Even when Shep, the farm collie, makes a frantic dash across the field, chug-sug senses the danger in time to make a reasonably unhurried retreat to his burrow.

He's a shrewd animal in spite of his seeming unconcern with human affairs. His underground burrow may go to a depth of five feet and is often twenty to thirty feet in length. One side of the burrow terminates in a blind sac, and here he builds a comfortable grass nest. Usually he also has a secret "plunge" hole, dug from within so that there is no telltale mound of fresh earth to reveal its location. Contrary to general opinion, chug-sug can climb a tree and is a good swimmer if an emergency arises.

On autumn mornings when the air is chilly and mists rise as the sun's rays strike the cold earth, the woodchuck pokes around the clover patch for a few nibbles of food. He almost waddles in his thick fat, for he's nearly ready for winter's sleep.

98

When the lashing cold storms come, he'll be curled snugly in his bed. His blood grows cooler and cooler; his pulse slows to a few beats a minute. For weeks he sleeps in the miracle state we label hibernation. But in late February or early March we'll see his tracks again, and the countryman will know that winter's back is broken.

DIGGING POTATOES

DIGGING potatoes by hand is one of the annual jobs on a farm. A lad can think of many more interesting things to do, but he'd much prefer to be digging potatoes than spreading manure or cleaning out the hen house. It's reasonably hard work, not so interesting perhaps as stacking beans but definitely above pulling turnips. For one thing, a boy can work with a tool, and as he will be the first to admit, if a fellow can work with something in his hands like an ax, or reins, or a potato digger, it's a notch above handwork.

It's fun of a sort to drive the long tines of the digger beneath the ridged hills and pull the nest of potatoes out. In the fall, if there's been a good frost and the tops of the plants are completely wilted and brown, it's just the matter of a jiffy to pull them off and toss them out of the way. There's a satisfying sense of accomplishment as one works back and forth across the patch and sees the rows of clean-looking potatoes drying in the sun.

In the back of a lad's mind, however, are thoughts of the other part of the job. Each potato that rolls in the trough between the rows means a potato that has to be picked up later in a basket. Then the baskets must be emptied into the burlap bags. That's the afternoon's main job. It's a bit discouraging to a fellow on a Saturday afternoon when the Black Pirates have a game scheduled against the Bloody Buccaneers. Somehow, the countryman senses the impending crisis, though, and appears at just the right time to lend his help. By four o'clock the good potatoes are all bagged and the small ones put in a pile to be cooked in the old iron kettle for the pigs. And when a young man dashes away with restored strength to play football, the farmer contentedly hoists the bags to the farm wagon and carries them to the woodshed where they'll dry out a few days before they are stored in the cellar.

HEARTH TENDING

THE leaping flames and steady song of a fireplace have an ageless appeal to man. He who would be a good hearth tender must be patient and cheerful, a dreamer and a philosopher. It isn't given to all men to be good keepers of the hearth. There are spotless housekeepers who dislike the spilling embers. Tolerance is needed in most phases of human activity, but particularly in this one of hearth tending.

One requires, first of all, a good deep bed of ashes. When they top the firedogs, a man has something to work with. He can bed his big backlog in them, and as the other sticks take hold, the glowing top layer of ashes sends a steady heat into the room. A fireplace that is cleaned daily is nothing but a quick wood consumer. There is considerable argument among countrymen as to the best kindling for starting a fire. Some prefer finely split birch; others use small pine limbs; and still others think bark pieces or wadded newspapers are best.

A man cherishes his logs as he gently lowers them to their sacrifice. Oak and hickory burn with a clear golden flame. White birch throws a hot, generous heat and orange-red streaks that make changing patterns in the deep yellow body of fire. Maple has a reddish hue in its steady flames and a blue-gray base. It burns quietly with no crackles and few sparks. Elm has one of the loveliest of all flames—a pure russet red—and when the burning is done, there is a log replica of beautiful white ashes marked in squares and rectangles. Spruce and hemlock are the political orators of the fireplace. They argue, shout, and bluster. They throw sparks onto the rug as their bright red flames, outlined with streaks of steel gray, leap upward. Apple wood flames are the most beautiful of all. The wood burns evenly; the colors are a symphony of red, orange, blue, and soft shades of gray; a pungent spicy fragrance spreads through the room.

Yes, when autumn comes, a man must look to his hearth tending. A fireplace has a utilitarian value, but its chief purpose is to help a man dream his dreams.

WALKING WEATHER

WHEN the last few leaves are dropping from maples, beeches, elms, and birches, when the slow-flowing woodland brooks are no longer concealed by a moist carpet of golds, reds, and browns, the year's best walking weather is at hand. In the hill country of the northland the pasture oaks cling to their faded brown, leathery foliage. Hillsides and hardwood ridges are temple groves for a brief time each sunny day, as shafts of gold light make patterns among the tree trunks and on the fresh-fallen ground cover.

Between leaf-dropping time and Indian summer comes an interlude of bracing days and tingling nights. Each morning white hoarfrost lies on meadows and fields. The fall plowing is a mass of little icy crinkles and ravines. As the late-rising sun sends its slanting ray over a chilled world, the light calls forth miniature jewel gleams for a few moments. Small ponds of mist gather in the lowlands and hesitatingly dissolve into nothingness as the morning wears on. Wisps of mist play over the dark, damp wooden shingles on weathered springhouses and gray-boarded barns.

It's good to walk on the land in late October. There's a crispness in the air whether the sun shines or stratus clouds cast a gray hue over the valleys and mountains. When the leaves have fallen from alders and sumacs, and the goldenrod and asters droop toward the ground, one can see the etched lichen pictures on the stone walls. The great heaps of stones in the corners of upland fields look like piles of big gray apples. The yellow-tan soil before the woodchuck dens makes dots by the pasture fence.

From an upland lookout one can see far. White church spires make exclamation points among village elms; the river winding through the brown valley floor is a crooked silver thread. On a clear night when the countryman climbs to the top of the steep pasture, it seems as if the sky were an inverted bowl flecked with golden dots. This is walking weather at its best. It brings man in closer touch with verities that offer solace in a troubled world.

ONE of the interesting points about food is that people have so many definite ideas concerning it. At the risk of being labeled old-fashioned, the countryman would like to say a few words about one of the happiest combinations yet devised. Bread may be the staff of life, but Americans decided some time ago it shouldn't be eaten alone—or with just butter. Bread has become something on which one eats peanut butter, jelly, jam, preserves, marmalade, maple sugar, maple syrup—or molasses.

There was a time, not too long ago, when molasses basked in the popularity it really deserves. The general store—"Groceries, Meats, Provisions, Hardware, Clothing, and Grains"— wouldn't have been a genuine store unless it had a big hogshead of molasses sitting on the sturdy frame of four-by-fours in the back room. In those days farm and village families brought in earthen gallon jugs to be filled with the brownish-black, thick, gooey, gloriously sweet liquid. Molasses was a staple product. It was needed for Indian puddings, gingerbread, half a dozen kinds of cookies; it was used on buckwheat cakes and on fried cornmeal mush. It gave the intangible but exhilarating life to baked beans. Mother had a molasses cake that rated above her famous thirteen-egg sponge affair—in the opinion of a boy.

There was another use for molasses. When a bread-baking came from the oven, and Mother cut an inch-thick slice of the white, steaming, fragrant loaf with its brown, crunchy crust, spread on golden butter with lavish generosity, and then poured molasses over the whole thing, it was food for a hungry boy.

A GOOD deal has been written and much has been said about house cellars with their rows of colorful glass jars of fruits and vegetables, pickles, preserves, jams, and jellies. But scarce has been the comment and scant the praise of root cellars. They are unsung, plebeian affairs, as earthy and indigenous to the countryside as the materials from which they are made.

The countryman is proud of his root cellar. It has a peculiar appeal and meaning in the cycle of the seasons. Probably its origins trace back to the dim eras when nomadic tribes ceased their wanderings and settled down to be husbandmen. No one knows when man first began to dig holes in the earth or to make excavations in hillsides for storage places. Probably the first root cellars were natural caves in hills and mountains.

Here in the New World the pioneers built their root cellars soon after their log cabins and log barns were notched up from the trees that came from clearing the land. There's nothing pretentious about them. A good-sized hole was dug in a hillside or at the back of a garden. The walls, at first of logs, were later replaced with stone and mortar. When men began to bake bricks of native clay, they were used for the walls in many areas. Often the roofs were peaked affairs of heavy planks.

It is cool, moist, and dark inside. Wide shelves hold cabbages and boxes of fancy Northern Spies, Blue Pearmains, and Russets. Bins are full of potatoes, carrots, beets, and turnips. There's a grand smell in an old root cellar, heady, pungent, and deeply satisfying, compounded of moist earth, old wood and vegetables. Root cellars are becoming old-fashioned in these days when we are learning to freeze and dehydrate our food for use against the time of cold. However, they once played a faithful, humble role in man's economy.

BREAKFASTS

ADMITTEDLY there are many things wrong with the present social order. Garages aren't big enough for a car and two bicycles; hall closets are overstuffed; folding chairs collapse unpredictably; and womenfolks keep moving the living-room furniture around. But if the countryman were pressed to hazard a guess as to what ails society most, he would venture the opinion that we need to eat bigger breakfasts to level off some of our bumpy waves.

Noah Webster is right in order in his usual terse, impersonal way when he states that breakfast is the first meal of the day. He doesn't talk about a doughnut and a cup of coffee, or a glass of juice and a slice of dry toast. He calls the first eating session a meal. Now that we're eighty per cent urban in a nation of one hundred forty-three million, the cause of breakfast trouble may be that people don't have cows to milk, pigs to feed, and chickens to look after between the time they get up and the day's first meal. When a man does chores for an hour or two before he eats, he can work up a pretty respectable appetite.

In our form of society everyone is entitled to his own ideas. The best breakfast is a matter of opinion. After years of extensive observation and careful experimentation, the countryman has finally worked out a combination that suits him per-

105

fectly. He wants a hot cereal with cold juicy applesauce, two eggs sunny side up, a couple of pieces of bacon, two thick slices of toast from homemade bread with coatings of butter and elderberry jelly, plenty of honest coffee, plus a piece of pie and a few gingersnaps to tamp it down.

There are men of calm judgment who prefer several brown-crusted hot biscuits with plenty of raspberry jelly. Others with pioneering appetites claim that a small piece of beefsteak and a baked potato or a good slice of tangy ham and a few crisp fried potatoes are an excellent foundation for a forenoon's labor. A man can make his choice. The point is that with a good meal in the morning he is ready to face unpredictable events in the course of the day with optimism and equanimity.

HUNTING EGGS

THE countryman readily admits that the intelligence quotient of the average hen tends toward the low side. Anyone who has tried to drive a hen in a straight line will corroborate that point of view. But there's something about a hen that gives her an affectionate place in a man's regard. A hen never talks back except in an optimistic vein. She is always glad to see a man when he comes into the pen. She sings her alto song when she's making up her mind to lay an egg and cackles for a few minutes after she has accomplished the feat.

On modern poultry farms everything is very scientific, with ultraviolet lights, running water, cod-liver oil, and a plethora of vitamins. But on many a farm a small flock of hens has the run of the yard and barn. Only an occasional egg is expected

in the wintertime. But in spring and summer the hens fly into
the mows and onto the scaffolds; they hide their nests behind
the machinery in the tool shed and in dark corners of the grain
room and the unused calf pens.

From mid-March on, hunting eggs is a daily task for a young
man. As soon as warm weather comes some of the hens find
secluded spots along the stone walls, in the tangle of blackberry vines behind the icehouse, and in the lilac hedge at the
end of the woodshed. Usually a lad discovers the nests before
a hen goes broody and begins her three-week vigil. Sometimes
a hen is successful and on a summer day comes proudly forth
with a flock of baby chickens. Nothing very exciting or mo-
mentous by the gauge of contemporary goings on. But for
generations farm boys and girls have enjoyed the day-to-day
game with the biddies. Hunting eggs is one of the pleasant
and essential tasks that makes farm life interesting.

BROWN BANNERS

FALL is the season of year when slender cattails lift their
brown cylindrical banners and sway with dignified grace in
the autumn winds. One finds them around the shores of
marshy-edged ponds, in the pasture swamps, and in the wet
soil along the sloughs that band sluggish-flowing creeks and
brooks. *Typha latifolia* lives up to its name: *typha* means bog
and *latifolia* broad-leaved. As with many widely distributed
plants, it enjoys many folklore names: cat-o'-nine-tails, cattail
flag, bull seg, water torch, and candlewick. The English call
it the reed mace and use the long flat leaves for seating chairs.

In June and July the countryman likes to watch the cattails in blossom. The upper half of the bloom is much narrower than the lower. The staminate flowers are massed at the top, while the pistillate flowers that form the banner are at the bottom. As the weeks of hot weather pass, the soft-furred olive-yellow flowers gradually disappear in wind and rain, and when the nights begin to grow crisp and frosty, the familiar reddish-brown cylinders are held aloft.

In October one sees the groups of pennants in moist fens and bogs. With their light brown leaves and sturdy stems they blend with the frost-seared marsh grasses that surround them and the golden-tan grass blankets that cover meadows and mowing fields. Often the leaves are taller than the blooms and make a graceful background. In the late afternoon as a farmer finishes plowing the field near the low end of the pasture, he likes to stand a minute and look at the cattails in the swamp on the other side of the wall. He knows that when winter comes and the snow lies deep over the land, they will still be there—lifting brown banners to the gray skies.

BLUE JAY

THERE are two schools of thought about this handsome member of the bird family. Some condemn him outright and see no good in him at all. The blue jay does deserve most of the derogatory remarks that have been directed his way. When he establishes his claim over a section, the other birds give him a wide berth. He's a thief and a robber; he's domineering and seems to enjoy a quarrel. He shatters the peace of the brooding autumn countryside with his raucous and penetrating screams.

But having said the worst about him, there are those who point out that Nature has her own mysterious system of checks and balances. The blue jay is just one part of the total scheme. Therefore, why not enjoy the good points of *Cyanocitta cristata?* His gorgeous coat rivals the best outfit of a drum major. His blue body is a beautiful shade of ultramarine. His crest is a deeper blue, which he flaunts like the top gear of a potentate's palace guard. His wings and tail are exquisitely barred with black and white. All his tail feathers except the middle two have broad bands of white.

It would help, of course, if "Blue Boy" would purge his vocabulary. He screams and rants; he shouts expletives in bird language; he scolds and grumbles. Undoubtedly his disposition is cantankerous and unpredictable. But when he's in a good mood he's a totally different individual. He's a grand mimic and a ventriloquist of above-average ability. He delights in imitating the impatient "meow" of the catbird. And then a moment later he gives forth with a few sweet notes of surprising bell-like tones.

In spite of his truculent, extrovert personality and his rough treatment of smaller birds, the countryman is rather fond of him. As days grow shorter, the blue jays grow louder. They flash like blue meteors through the woods, screaming that fall is on the way. They haunt the oak trees and tear acorns apart. They dash around the farm buildings and blast the dog and the cat with staccato chatterings. They're the bad boys of the bird family, but the countryside wouldn't seem natural without them.

IN a period of contemporary fretting over the position of the hem line and other such matters, the countryman is somewhat diffident about bringing up the subject. But when a news item categorically states that the best sweet cider is made from the McIntosh, it is time for a public airing of the issue.

One doesn't say that good cider cannot be made from the sport apple tree that a Scotchman in Canada developed into a variety. If the Macs are picked early while they still have zip and zest, a very good liquid indeed can be extracted. After long experimentation and impartial tasting, however, this statement can be made: the best cider is a blend in equal proportions of Baldwins, Northern Spies, and Blue Pearmains. The liquid is amber-gold in color; it is not too sweet. In it one gets a hint of spring rains in apple-blossom time, the memory of the hot heart of summer and the crisp headiness of white-frost October nights.

Sweet cider is important in its own right, but a countryman also has in mind boiled cider to furnish the base of apple butter. Too few cooks know that a modicum of apple butter in baked beans is a touch of magic. Too few city folks realize that spicy apple butter has a natural affinity for yellow-meal johnnycake, brown-crusted biscuits, and thick chewy slices of toast. Sweet cider is the essential foundation of prime apple butter, and some happy day the bland, brown goodness will come into its own again. The old-fashioned apple varieties are gradually disappearing, but wise farmers will keep a few trees to produce a sweet cider that really satisfies.

NOVEMBER

NOVEMBER is an in-between season in Nature's calendar. The time of fulfillment has come and gone; months of warmth and rain have meant the cycle of planting, cultivation, and harvest. Now the year's clock is slowly and inexorably running down. Days follow one another in brown quietness. For long periods the stratus clouds hang low over fields, pastures, and hills. Brown grass carpets the meadows and mowings, and brown is the moist, soft rug in the woodland beneath the maples and oaks.

Toward the end of the "mad-moon" month white hoar-frost glistens in the mornings as the sun's slanting rays stretch outward from the rim of the east. There's a damp sheen on the brown ribbons of freshly plowed soil. Pearl-gray smoke spirals upward from farmhouse chimneys and drifts away in lateral banners that gradually dissolve into nothingness. Late-staying birds gather in flocks and go swirling over the fields and gardens; squirrels hustle in frantic haste to build a few more caches against the lean times ahead. Crows sit around in the trees above the pasture spring or meet in small groups on the stubble in the mowing field, discussing current events in a desultory fashion.

The countryman finds plenty to do in the eleventh month. Work isn't exactly pressing on the farm, but a man likes to check his buildings to see that they are tight against the arrows of sleet and rain that are sure to come. Corn shocks are hauled near the barn; the hen house is cleaned and spread with fresh, crisp straw. The garden has to be raked up and left shipshape for spring. Whatever a man can do in the fall means a head-start in the new year. Day's end comes quickly; no slow drawing of the curtain. There's a biting chill to the air. A period of Indian summer, perhaps. Days of mellowness occasionally. But November is the prelude to winter.

COUNTRY-SCHOOL LUNCHES

BEFORE the age of vitamins, scientifically balanced meals, and lettuce leaves for winter food, boys and girls trudged to the country school at the crossroads carrying a two-quart lard pail full of substantial food. Doubtless modern nutritionists righteously bristle when they think of the solid, heavy lunch that tasted so good to hungry youngsters. All morning long in cold weather the pails sat in a row on the shelf at the front of the schoolroom. In spring and fall they sat on the floor beneath coats and hats in the front entryway.

When a fellow took off the tin cover at noon, he knew he had a real meal ahead of him. The foundation was three or four thick sandwiches of crusty, chewy homemade bread generously covered with butter he had probably helped to churn. But the butter was only a taken-for-granted part of the filling. Likely there were succulent slices of roast pork or roast beef between the bread. Perhaps there would be one sandwich with lots of blackberry jam. It oozed around the edges and colored the bread a rich, satisfying purple.

All this was good, but merely a preliminary introduction to the desserts. A hungry, growing boy, like his father, wanted a

114

big wedge of pie, a man-sized piece of walnut cake, a couple of large oatmeal cookies, and perhaps an apple or two to top things off. It was always possible to do a little dickering with one's friends and get a doughnut for a couple of cookies, or a second piece of cake for the apples. Lard-pail lunches are part of the background of many men and women now far from farms and rural schools. They would not satisfy modern dietitians, but not too long ago when school recessed for an hour at twelve o'clock, they served well the purposes for which farm mothers packed them.

ELEVENTH-MONTH SECRETS

GONE now is the foliage from the maples and birches, the elms and willows; gone are the leaves from the thick-growing alders along the meadow brook and from the cherries, sumacs, and high-bush blueberries that have half concealed the old stone walls. The goldenrod and wild asters are grayed and flattened by black frosts and pelting rains. In the pasture swamps the tall ranks of coarse-bladed grasses are bending low over the black pools and mossy hummocks.

The orioles' nests swing like gray mittens from the pendulant branches of the elms, and the robins' mud-caked homes are half broken in the branches of the apple trees behind the barn. Down by the brook one can see the nests of the warblers and the vireos. In the reedy area between the meadow and the pasture one may, if one searches diligently, find the nest of the pair of bitterns whose hoarse, thumping calls sounded in the June twilight.

Along the stone walls one can now see the piles of earth where the woodchucks dug their dens last spring. Along the meadow brooks are the runways of the muskrats. A path leads from the big pool where the deer come to drink to their winter yard in the spruce woods. Above the rocky pasture the old sugar maples stand gaunt and rugged. Here and there among the branches are the tumbled leafy nests of the gray squirrels. From the slender branches of a white birch a big gray conical hornets' nest moves back and forth in the breeze.

On a bright, cloudless, late November day there's a peculiar quality of light. Hills across the valley seem close and distinct. The river winds like a gleaming silver thread between the brown meadows. The houses across the fields and in the village seem very near. Bare trees stand against the sky like detailed etchings. November is a revealing month—a month of disclosures before the snows come to cover autumn's brown and tattered quilt.

KEROSENE LAMPS

SOMEDAY a scholar will write a history of man's development in terms of the lights he has used. In such a story the humble kerosene lamp will receive due recognition. It was an epochal day when someone conceived the idea that a frame of glass would steady the flame and diffuse the light. Those who live in areas served by electricity sometimes forget that there are millions of people who still use lamps and lanterns.

On oilcloth-covered shelves above kitchen sinks the hand lamps stand. A spotless, shining chimney is the mark of a good

116

housewife. Through the generations they have lighted the way up narrow stairs at bedtime. They have stood on shelves behind big kitchen stoves while farm wives prepared winter breakfasts before sunup; and as early dusk fell on midwinter afternoons, the small lamp has rested on its shelf above the kitchen table while the biscuits were beaten for supper.

The hand lamp was the Martha of light givers. After supper was eaten on the big table with its red-and-white checked cloth, the milking done and animals bedded for the night, dishes washed and the batter for buckwheat cakes stirred down, the big lamp with its painted glass shade was set in the middle of the eating table. In its soft, gentle light, boys and girls did their home-work, pored over the mail-order catalogues, and dreamed youth's dreams of a world to conquer. Father sat in the old Morris chair and read the city paper and the farm journals by the light of another small lamp on the table to which geraniums and begonias were moved, away from frost-endangered windows. Mother, gently rocking, mended or knitted. The lamps that served the others gave light enough for her practiced fingers.

The parlor lamp was a thing of special beauty. Rarely used, it stood in polished and dusted splendor in the dim, austere front room, a sign that the house was properly furnished when the minister came to call. It was tall and ornate with complicated scrolls and curlicues around the base and stem. The shade was a colorful affair of violets and roses. Kerosene lamps, plebeian and utilitarian, have not only been light givers; but they have also helped satisfy man's love of beauty.

118

THERE was a time when choosing a new horse blanket was a major matter on the farm. A countryman didn't have too many opportunities to express his yearning for color. He could paint the democrat a deep blue and have narrow stripes of red or yellow for decoration; he could buy a buggy whip with a scarlet tassel. He could wear red galluses and a tie of moderate authority. But when it came to getting a new horse blanket, a man had a chance to unleash his hidden yearnings.

Naturally the whole family discussed the matter after supper. When the chores were done, the supper dishes washed, and the kitchen redded up, the kerosene lamps lighted, and the mail-order catalogues spread on the eating table, the discussion waxed vehement. Sisters who had arrived at the age where the blendings of colors were important argued for a plain brown blanket with perhaps a few stripes of tan. They wanted something discreet and artistic. Mother was willing to go as far as a modest check.

But Father and a twelve-year-older were adamant. They knew what they wanted. It had to be emphatic, authoritative, and colorful. The names were fascinating: "Redbird Fancy Plaid, Improved Apache Square, Lulu Fancy Striped, Great Eastern Fawn, and Rockaway Fancy Plaided." It did something to a fellow to read, "Wine-colored body with rich deep heading of old gold, blue, lemon, black, and white, with body stripes of the same colors." Or "Green body plaided with black, orange, tan, green, and white with combination blended heading of wine, orange, white, and green."

Ah, yes, choosing a horse blanket was a serious matter. There were too many colors and combinations. From a couple of dozen it was hard to make the final choice. But at length it was agreed. It was to be a Hudson plaid—green and brown, green plaid on one side and brown plaid on the other, with white and red small plaid through the body. "Very horsy," the advertisement said, "a blanket that will be very pleasing to the eye."

GRAVY CONSERVATION

THE time has come for good men to rally around the banner and do something about gravy sopping. We are in hearty accord with the general rules of etiquette. Standards are needed to guide us in the increasing complexity of human relationships—which include breaking bread together. We can, if necessary, tolerate red cherries perched precariously on salads; we are willing to abide by the general custom of eating desserts last, instead of first when one's taste buds are keenest. We can survive if some women fail to put raisins in their chocolate bread pudding.

When it comes to the matter of getting the last drop of good gravy from his plate, however, the countryman yields to no one in his insistence on the principles involved. Admittedly there's a divergence of opinion. Some men get their gravy by judicious use of mashed potatoes; others prefer to double a slice of well-buttered homemade bread and use this as a mopper-upper. There are those who cling tenaciously to johnnycake. It may be a bit crumbly but it can be patted into a fork-load when it has absorbed a part of the gravy.

After comprehensive cogitation and considerable personal experimentation, the countryman has come to the conclusion that nothing quite equals the all-around efficacy of a hot, buttered half of a cream-o'-tartar biscuit. It is a comfortable tool to handle and is highly efficient if it has a crisp, crunchy crust. With it a man can corner the gravy in a bend of the plate. A normal biscuit half is good for two bites—each well soaked with the flavorful, satisfying juices.

Etiquette books are all right in their place. But someday a practical tome will be compiled that will frankly, honestly, and complacently face the fact that a man is going to have his gravy in this life—and the book will offer practical suggestions for getting it without leaving spots on a clean tablecloth or a man's tie.

FARM DINNER BELLS

THERE are not many of them left now, but a generation ago the old dinner bell was a necessity on the farm. Sometimes it was placed on a red-cedar post by the ell door, its iron frame fitting onto the top of the pole and its short rope hanging above the reach of mischievous boys and girls. Sometimes it was fastened to the top of the springhouse or to the limb of a big maple in the yard, or perhaps it hung from a cross timber of the porch. Some farms had big hand bells that sat on the end of the oilcloth-covered shelf above the sink, beside the kerosene lamps.

121

If, by chance, a new bell was needed it was a matter for careful decision. Around the red-and-white checked kitchen table the family discussed it. The mail-order catalogue's descriptions were explicit. Should it be the "big 83¢ bell—large and handsome, of crystalline metal"? It weighed 37½ pounds and was full-bronzed. As the catalogue said, "At our extremely low price, but a shade above the actual value of the raw material, there is no reason why any farm should be without one of our large farm bells." Or would it be better to spend $2.35 for a 100-pound bell on a frame that could sit on the woodshed roof? This bell was "well finished, of extra fine tone, can be heard farther than any copper or tin bell of five times the cost, and is far more durable."

At noon the clear calls of the bells floated across fields and pastures, and over the countryside men and boys headed homeward for the midday meal. Each farm bell had its own distinctive tone. When a bell rang its measured toll at eleven-thirty, men looked up and said, "Guess Joe and his wife are going to eat early and go to town." Then there was the occasional tragic time when a bell rang frantically and neighbors rushed to a farm home to offer succor in an emergency.

Only a few bells are left on farms today, but men and women who live in cities and listen to chimes strike the hours remember the days when the bells along valley and hill roads rang out the time at high twelve of day.

ON a stormy Saturday in early winter when work in the barns and sheds was caught up, Father was likely to say after breakfast, "Son, why don't you take those pieces of harness to the village and get them mended? If Bill doesn't think that old trace is worth mending, tell him to give you a new one."

After the Morgan mare was hitched in the horseshed behind the town hall, blanketed, and given a lump of sugar, a lad draped harness pieces over his shoulder and headed for the harness shop. Boys were there from other farms; farmers had dropped in on their way to the grain mill; villagers had come to pass the time of day. The small one-room building was heated by a cast-iron stove, and the rusty stove pipe made a detour around the ceiling to give additional heat in cold weather. New, glistening harnesses hung from pegs on one side; old, worn, and broken pieces littered the floor. The windows were grimy and dusty; cobwebs were thick over them. In the corners were tangled piles of old pieces of harness: buckles, traces, breech straps, choke straps, hames, and collars. On long shelves at the rear were pieces of leather from which the harness maker cut parts.

The smell was an integral part of the shop. When a hot fire was going, it helped to emphasize the satisfying aroma compounded of oil, new leather, old harnesses, and dust. It was a heavy, pungent, satisfying fragrance, and on a day of lashing rain the smell was at its best. A harness shop was an important institution in the countryside's economy. It was a place of business. But more than that, it was a spot where a lad could spend a few pleasant hours, listening to men discuss the affairs of the local community and the outside world—a world into which a boy dreamed he would go one day and take his place.

MEPHITIS

THE skunk isn't a bad chap to know. His reputation, based on scent, does not do him justice. Anyone who has seen a mother skunk lead her brood of little ones in single file across a lawn at dusk, each tiny fellow with his tail held aloft like a banner, has seen one of the most appealing sights in Nature's living museum.

As man has cleared a home in the New World, some forms of wildlife have retreated to the swamps and the mountains; others have been eliminated entirely. But the skunk, like the fox and the opossum, has learned to survive in farm areas. Indeed, he can frequently be found, or smelled, in urban centers. It may be that *Mephitis* likes the company of man in spite of the way he has been persecuted.

He is a good friend of the farmer, though he makes an occasional foray on the chicken coop. He eats tremendous quantities of May beetles and their grubs; he consumes many of the field mice which eat the bark of trees, the heads of timothy, and the grains of oats, wheat, and buckwheat. Repeated surveys by biologists have proved that "Striped Suit" more than pays his way.

The common opinion is that *Mephitis* is a lethargic, stolid chap. While he seems indolent and slothful if he comes forth in the daylight hours, he's a changed being on a cool, moonlit autumn evening. Then he's active and nimble as he hustles

124

about in the crisp air, flipping stones to one side as he hunts for a grub or digs in the soil for a beetle or worm.

When the time of cold arrives, he goes into semihibernation in a rabbit or woodchuck hole, beneath an old building, or occasionally in a burrow he has dug himself. The countryman has a folklore saying that if skunks come around the farm buildings in numbers during the fall, it means a long, hard winter. *Mephitis* has a drawback in polite society, but he sets a good example for man in sobriety of action and strict attention to his own affairs if the world leaves him alone.

CORRECT WAY TO EAT PIE

MR. WEBSTER was chary of adjectives and adverbs; his statements are terse and impersonal. But in the countryman's opinion Noah was far off course when it came to pie. There's disappointing brevity in his definition: "An article of food consisting of a pastry crust with any of various kinds of filling; also a kind of layer cake spread with jam or cream." Disregarding the colossal nonsense of the latter half of the definition (no cake can logically be called a pie), it is depressing to think a man would dismiss the subject so casually.

Even more dampening to the spirit of one who believes that pies come at the head of the list of desserts is the fact that no mention is made of the correct way to eat them. It makes no difference what kind of pie is set before a man: apple, mince (hot or cold), cherry, strawberry, raspberry, rhubarb, raisin, apricot, lemon, squash (maple flavored), pumpkin, custard, chocolate, cranberry, vinegar, molasses, or caramel. We need

125

a national organization — a STHBCPC: Society to Teach Human Beings to Consume Pie Correctly. Most people begin this operation with the point of the wedge toward them. This is completely and unequivocably erroneous. There's only one technique to consuming a piece of pie in a civilized and intelligent fashion. Have the tip pointing diametrically away from one. Start with the outside crust first. If one gets rid of this part before beginning on the inside of the pie, the last forkload can be calculated nicely, and a man ends his meal with a good big mouthful of the filling. No matter what the etiquette books assert, this is the way to enjoy the inherent goodness of pie.

LATE NOVEMBER SUNSETS

THERE is a poignant time of hesitancy just before the browns of November give way to the grays of the twelfth month. Squaw winter has flung its introduction over the land. Snow showers have dusted brown fields and upland pastures. Ice sheets have temporarily covered the pools in the swamps. The preliminary cold spells have crocheted lacy lines along the brooks and creeks. Indian summer has brought its days of peaceful warmth, and Earth has relaxed from the first tentative assault.

During the period before winter's main forces move down from the north there are sunsets of beauty. The gold ball of the sun falls toward the mountain rim in a sky of washed blue. If atmospheric conditions are favorable, the canvas of the sky is painted a pattern of scarlets, gold, violets, and orange. It's not a canvas of spreading panorama, as in midsummer, when the

126

flaming colors reach toward the pole of the horizon. November's sunset pictures are smaller in size and the colors tend toward softer shades.

Often the colors run horizontally instead of vertically. There are long pennants of gold and soft reds above the hills. Occasionally there's a rare canvas of many shades of yellow without any deeper colors. If there are thin stratus clouds hanging low above the heights, one occasionally sees a concentration of reds, scarlets, and maroons that reminds one of an August sunset. Perhaps the loveliest of all November sunset pictures is the brief interlude of flaming glory when bare trees on the upland ridges are silhouetted against the colored sky. Then the trunks and branches of the oaks, beeches, and maples are sharply limned etchings. He who is sensitive feels the lonesome beauty of the scene. Late November sunsets are Nature's extra dividends before she posts her book for the year.

LOW TWELVE

NOW Earth is in her deep sleep and the hour hand of the year's clock draws close to low twelve. Gray shades hang low; the voice of cold is heard in the land. There are dry brittle cracklings along the rivers and creeks and sudden sharp reports when the sheet ice in the swamps breaks from the sides of mounded hummocks and reveals for a brief interlude the cold black water beneath.

Muffled are the sounds of the countryside. Soft and poignantly muted is the tone of the bell in the village clock as the tolling of the hours spreads over the deeply covered landscape. Gray is the air and faint the noise of the woodsman's ax in the wood lot on the hillside. A dog's bark from across the valley is lonesome sounding in the shadowy day. The chickadees in the old orchard behind the barn chant their refrains less often. Only occasionally does the blue jay call from the sugar grove.

The trees are waiting out the time. After a soft snow the evergreens wear mantles of white, and the maples, beeches, and oaks hold out white arms in patient supplication to the God of Winter. On the hilltops and mountain brows the bare trees lift their stark limbs in etched designs against the dark gray sky. And when the short December day draws to a close, deep dusk falls suddenly over the fields and hills, and the long night settles in. Men go about the farmyards with lanterns, and long thin shadows move on the snow and over the barns and corn cribs. Now time approaches the heart of winter. It is low twelve on Nature's clock.

129

IT's a peculiarly typical American custom to eat most on the day that one does the least. Here and there in the press, one occasionally comes upon items indicating there are those among the population who question the solidly entrenched tradition. By and large, however, the Sunday dinner is as much a part of the scene Americana as hot dogs, peanuts in the shell, and bottles of pop. Since this is a generally accepted fact, a few matters need to be called to attention.

The basis of the meal, of course, should be a big, juicy, tender, succulent roast of beef or lamb, or a large roast chicken. There are complications when Junior and Sally, Grandmother and Uncle Ed, all want the outside slices of the roast. When more than two want a drumstick, Father has to keep in mind who had the legs last time. If Junior and Sally get into an argument over the matter, for the sake of discipline it may be necessary for Father to say, "Well, since you cannot agree, just this once Mother and I will have the drumsticks."

The countryman has learned that often his favorite desserts come with Sunday dinner. His strategy is not to be recommended without some reservations in the light of the Golden Rule. Nevertheless, he has found that if the family and guests can be induced to eat seconds all around on the meat and vegetables, rolls and pickles, there's likely to be enough of the dessert left so that he can have an additional piece of pie or chocolate cake late in the evening. Theoretically, he should not resort to such connivings, but as any man knows who has two or more growing children, he has to think far ahead to make sure of his share of the desserts.

130

Sunday dinner is a good, solid institution; it's a welder of family unity and a generator of an appraising, sane outlook on a chaotic world.

NIGHT VISIT TO THE BARN

THERE is something about a good farmer and his feeling for his livestock that is difficult to express in words. It has been said that the eye of the true husbandman is an important yardstick when it comes to keeping the cattle in good bloom. Perhaps that is why many men follow a traditional ritual of a night visit to the barn.

The average countryman likes to go to bed early. The winter evenings follow a more or less standard pattern. The family gathers around the table and stove in the kitchen or else pulls the chairs in a half circle around the base-burner in the living room. While the young folks do their homework, read magazines, or look through the mail-order catalogues, Father goes through the daily papers, reads the farm journals or, during the late winter evenings, studies the seed catalogues. Maybe there is popcorn, and likely Father wants a dish of cold, juicy Northern Spies. But when it gets around nine o'clock, he puts on his overshoes, cap, and sheep-lined jacket, lights the kerosene lantern, and goes out for his night visit to the barn.

To a man who likes livestock, there is nothing else in the day's routine to compare to this last look around before going to bed. The work of the day is done. A man knows that the chances are ninety-nine to one that everything is safe and secure, but he could not go to bed easy in his mind unless he had made this last inspection. It is good to see the milkers in the tie-up. Most of them are lying down, chewing their cuds. They are well bedded in crisp straw or fresh, tangy sawdust. The horses, crunching on good clover and timothy, turn their heads to look at their master as he glances in the stalls to see that their halters are not twisted. The calves and young stock crowd to the gates of their pens for the caressing rub behind their ears they have come to expect.

All is calm and safe. As the countryman closes the barn door and walks across the snowy yard, the kerosene lantern throws long shadows on the dim whiteness. As he goes through the woodshed, the light glances at the ordered tiers of oak, maple, beech, and ash. Back in the cozy kitchen, he blows out the lantern and sets it on the shelf above the sink. The night visit to the barn is over. Now the farmstead can settle to rest.

PAPERMAKERS' NESTS

WINTER is a good time to see the papermakers' nests. Varying in length and diameter from a few inches to large cones two feet long, the silvery homes of the white-faced black hornets hang like etchings from the limbs of gray birches and wild cherries and make pictures against the gray sky. From the splintered surfaces of old boards, rails, and posts the hornets tear off bits of wood, which they reduce to pulp by mixing with saliva. Then they plaster the thin sheets on the outside of their cone-shaped homes.

The queen is the only member of the family that lives through the winter. Each spring she builds a little home and lays eggs. When the first members of the season's family arrive, they begin to enlarge the nest to accommodate the successive broods. As the clan increases, the paper is cut away from the inside and new layers are added to the outside. All summer long the housebuilding goes on.

The home of the papermakers is one of the wonders of the insect world. From a small cottage with few honeycombs in spring it may grow to a large nest by August. All summer it is the scene of bustling activity. When the freezing weather of late October brings black frosts to the land, all the papermakers except the queen of the tribe will have finished their cycle. The queen, in response to age-old instinct, crawls away to some protected spot to spend the winter. Then in the cold grayness of a cloudy, windy day the nests sway in the wind—reminders of Nature's never-ceasing cycle.

BARK PATTERNS

WINTER brings days when the light is peculiarly intense, days when the hills across the valley seem close and details stand forth that one doesn't notice in midsummer's fullness of foliage. That is true of the barks of trees, some of which have beautiful and distinctive patterns.

The sycamore, or buttonwood, is perhaps the most unusual of all our native species. Large cream-white blotches stand out distinctly with flecks of brown irregularly spaced against the light areas. The light-colored spots extend far up the trunks and out along the main branches. Groves of dignified beeches stand like Druid's temples on hillside openings, surrounded by spruces, pines, and hemlocks. The bark of the beech is smooth and a light steel gray with tiny dots of black. The ladies of the woodland, the slender, graceful white birches, are clothed in white robes with little lacy frills of bark curling from the trunk at intervals. The humble cousins of the white ladies, the gray birches, cluster along the stone walls, gather in fence corners, and hold meetings in open glades in the woods, their grayish-white bark set off by lines of brown-black stitching. The velvet sumac lifts its twisting, irregular limbs, and the smooth, soft hairs on the younger branches feel like silk against the brown-gray bark.

The countryman's favorite among the bark patterns is the sugar, or rock, maple. In the maple-sugar bush on the sidehill, among the lichen-covered granite boulders and the steep-sided, craggy ravines, the huge trees stand in friendly firmness. Their trunks are covered with rough, thick bark, on which green mosses grow. There are crevices and gullies in the bark and it's hard to the touch, but there's something about its gray-green stanchness that fits the rugged countryside. Each tree has its own pattern. For him who loves Nature in her myriad moods winter is a good time of year to study patterns in bark.

PENNY CANDY

THE countryman misses the cracker barrel in the general store; he believes it would be well to keep a big cheese on the counter so a man could slice himself a wedge while waiting for the five-fifteen to bring the mail from the city. He feels that we will not have the right kind of gingerbread until we get some of the old-fashioned tangy molasses that used to come in barrels. He regrets that the hulled-corn man no longer comes around in his pung.

However, the most distressing lack, and one that has a deleterious effect on the modern social order, is the scarcity of penny candy. A voting-age citizen who has never had the opportunity to choose a dime's worth of hard candies in a cluttered, dusty, rounded-glass candy counter is not properly prepared to cope with the contemporary scene. Buying penny candy taught life's important lessons. A lad learned to weigh all angles and to make his decision in the light of known results.

Pike's Peak chocolates were delicious at two for a cent, but they had no lasting quality. Gibraltars, rock candy of many flavors, hard mints, beer barrels, buttermels, druggist mints, candy cigarettes, and colored wafers not only had good flavor, but also they were so constituted that they lasted well in the mouth. In between recitation periods in the district school a lad could slip a piece under his tongue and keep up his strength until time to open the lunch bucket. A stick or two of licorice was long lasting and satisfactory. Boston baked beans and the sugar-coated peanuts had points in their favor, and a large chocolate cigar with a gold-paper band gave a young man a definite adult feeling.

The choosing of penny candies taught boys and girls to think. It may not be in keeping with the tempo of the era, but the countryman believes a penny-candy counter in the United Nations' headquarters and one in the halls of Congress might have salubrious results.

THE general stores in country villages and at four-corners hamlets serve the needs of a surprising number of families. It is heartening to read a news item that such stores are staging a comeback. And according to economics professors, one of the fundamental laws of commerce is that a successful business serves a need of mankind.

There is a good, wholesome, pungent fragrance in a general country store. It is compounded of aromas from kerosene, cheese, leather, candy, rubber footwear, woolen pants, common crackers, coffee, bolts of gingham, dust, and the heat from the big potbellied stove. Perhaps the store is not architecturally beautiful, but it is functionally efficient. On one side are the groceries and candies; on the other are the notions, yard goods, and women's wear. The heaped counter in the center is a confused jungle of men's pants, overalls, sheep-lined jackets, felt boots, leggings, and caps. Toward the back is a stove surrounded by a few broken chairs. On the rear wall is a conglomeration of small hardware, bits of harness, pitchforks, shovels, and rakes. Kegs of nails and bolts are on the floor. In the back room are stored the big drums of kerosene and molasses and a clutter of miscellaneous tools; in the shed beyond are the bags of grain and bales of hay.

Of course, the general store is a mart of business. But it is much more than that. It is a place where men gather to wait for the five-fifteen local from the city, where they meet to discuss and settle local, national, and international affairs. The general store deals in commercial affairs, but it also deals in democratic friendliness. It has played and is still playing its role in the drama of country living.

MANY men look out at gray December skies and think of the time when they helped get the Christmas tree. The day before Christmas Father was likely to say after breakfast, "Son, let's take our axes and go up to the wood lot. Mother and the girls will want to trim the tree this evening."

It was an anticipated annual ritual. After the chores were finished, the stock watered, the barns cleaned, and the horses currycombed, the countryman and a lad went up through the orchard of old Baldwins, Northern Spies, and Blue Pearmains, climbed the pasture, and went through the maple-sugar grove into the evergreen stretch above the hardwoods. Among the cedars, spruces, and hemlocks all was peaceful and quiet. It was as if they entered a world where strife and man-made problems were unknown. There was a gentle murmuring among the branches overhead. The air was filled with the tangy, invigorating fragrance of the evergreens.

Here and there in the woods were open glens and nooks. In these areas the younger trees were growing. "We want a tree just seven feet tall," Father would say. "It must be well shaped all around and have a good single spike at the tip for the Star of Bethlehem." It took a little searching to find just the right tree. "Nothing wrong about cutting a tree for Christmas," Father would continue, "if you take one where they are grow-ing together too thickly. Wood lots need thinning and pruning just like all other crops."

There was nothing spectacular or unusual about the scene —just a farmer and his son selecting a tree to help commemo-rate the time of peace on earth, good will to men. Through generations of time men and boys have gone forth with their axes. As a new nation has developed in the Western World, the green trees have been placed in humble farm homes. And the star at the top is a symbol that in the hearts of men is a dream of the time when wars and the rumors of war shall be gone forever. For peace on earth, good will to men is the Grail for which we seek.

BRANCH-LINE TRAIN

THE branch-line train was an important part of the valley's life. Each morning it came from the county seat and chugged and huffed its way through a dozen towns to the junction where folks could connect for the city. Late each afternoon it made the return trip. "Old 61" made the two trips a day for years. She was an ancient two-wheeler with a rusty cowcatcher. The one regular car was a combination baggage car and passenger coach. The seats in the passengers' section had red-plush coverings, and the brass of the kerosene lamps that hung above the aisle was always polished.

In the morning the baggage section was well filled with jugs of milk. Each evening the empties were returned. Many a farm lad was eager to drive the Morgan mare to the village depot in the late afternoon to pick up the milk jugs. There was something about gathering at the depot that made a chap feel he was a man of the world. It was just a branch-line depot—a small, gray, sooty building with a tall cast-iron stove inside. The depot master handled freight and express, and listened to the mysterious clacking of the telegraph key. By and by, "Old

61's" long, plaintive whistle would sound from down the line. "She's at Hubbard's crossing," he would say. "She's only ten minutes late tonight. Must be Bill is pushing her pretty hard." The old train always provided a thrill when she drew in with a hissing of steam, a clanging of the bell, and a squealing of brakes. There were shouts back and forth, the clanking of empty cans, perhaps a few boxes to be unloaded, among them a crate of fat chickens to be sent to the commission firm over at the county seat.

Unpretentious and not too efficient, yes. But over a nation boys and girls have listened to the whistles of branch-line trains and have resolved that some day they would be on those red-plush seats, riding off to meet life's high adventures.

THE LAMPLIGHTER

HE went along the village streets in late afternoon—a humble elderly man with a wheelbarrow, a stubby ladder, and a five-gallon can of coal oil. In little elm-shaded towns where white church spires pointed toward the stars, the iron-framed glass cages sat on cedar posts at regular intervals along the street. Fifty years ago when night's curtain dropped over hills and valleys, the lights along the village streets were a necklace of halo-edged golden beads, held taut on an invisible string.

Small boys were the lamplighter's faithful retinue. The work itself was routine: set the ladder, fill the lamp inside the cage, trim the wick, and light it. Once a week the old man polished the cages and chimneys with peculiarly gray-black cloths. "Don't know how old Ben keeps the lamps shining so

140

brightly," more than one good housewife has said. "Have you seen his cleaning cloths?"

To lads now grown to manhood and scattered over a nation there was much more to the daily task. Old Ben had been around in his youth. He knew the Western plains and Southern pinewoods; he had trapped on the frozen tundras and worked in Northern lumber camps. He had sailed around the world on a slow freighter. As he worked, he told wide-eyed youngsters stories of their own nation's history and interesting facts about the distant places of the world. Strange-sounding names in the geography books came alive as he painted word pictures of other peoples and places.

Ostensibly the lamplighter was just a humble man performing one of the community's housekeeping tasks, but he often fired the hearts of his listeners with ambition. Lamplighters no longer light lamps in glass cages, but the lights they kindled in many a boy's heart are still shining.

DECEMBER SOUNDS

THIS is the month of thin sounds. Winds whip up suddenly and subside abruptly. For the most part December's sounds are in keeping with the spirit of oncoming winter. Among the scrub oaks above the maple-sugar grove the brittle, bleached leaves rustle as the west wind passes by. The faded-gold, paper-thin leaves of the beeches around the pasture spring sound like the steady pattering of rain in a distant forest. Down in the creek bottom the ice-sheeted brook sings its muted music as the slow waters work downward to the sea.

Stand in the heart of the swamp on a cold late-December day and you will hear thin noises as ice deepens around reed-topped hummocks and muskrat domes. Now that Earth's breast is frozen and winter is ready to give the last turn to the key that locks the land, the birds have lowered their voices to the spirit of the season. The blue jays have ceased their screaming and only occasional clear-toned bugles mark their passage through the orchard. Chickadees tumble over tree trunks and repeat their names in a monotone key.

In midafternoon when a man finishes his day's chopping, it is good to stand and listen to the hushed murmuring of the evergreens above. The soft conversation of the pines, spruces, and hemlocks is keyed to the time of year. As one comes down the pasture slope, shadows have already covered the valley. The mountain peaks are a painting in shades of blues, lavenders, and deep reds. The sweet, thin notes of the bell in the village spire float slowly by. Quickly colors fade and darkness deepens.

FRYING DOUGHNUTS

THERE were times when a lad liked to work in reasonable proximity to the kitchen. His attitude toward splitting wood or stacking it in the woodshed, for example, could be influenced to a considerable degree by kitchen activities. Mondays and Tuesdays were the washing and ironing days, so they were not likely to pay dividends. But on other days, if advance indications were promising, it was profitable for a boy to come in occasionally with an armful of fuel for the wood box.

Sometimes it was difficult to make a decision. Would he prefer hot gingerbread fresh from the oven? Or would a couple of thick, crusty slices of freshly baked bread with plenty of butter and molasses be better? Another favorite was Mother's satisfying gingersnaps with a raisin in the center of each.

However, for all-around purposes a lad would vote first for hot, fragrant, golden-crusted doughnuts. There is something special about a hot doughnut. If it is made correctly with plenty of cream and butter, if it is fried for just the right length of time in fat of just the proper temperature, it stands alone as a reason why menfolks need to come into the kitchen during the forenoon. The aroma drifts through the summer kitchen to where a lad is chopping kindling wood in the shed. The fact that he has been told the doughnuts won't be ready for a long, long time is no help. When Father goes through the ell into the kitchen—to get a drink of water, of course,—a young man suddenly realizes he, too, is thirsty. When the doughnuts are finally ready and cool enough to take in his hands, the good smell is merely an advance notice of the delicious taste. About four or five of the hot, chewy, hole-encircling fried cakes and a glass or two of cold creamy milk make a very welcome mid-morning snack.

WHEN slow December has plodded through its gray days and the God of Gates and Entrances has mounted his throne for a month's rule, the countryman has a definite feeling that the year has started uphill to spring. There is beauty and satisfaction in the diminuendo pace from the end of October through the brownness that is November and the neutral hues that are the twelfth month. But there is something about the turn of the year that gives a lift to human hearts.

The sun has turned again toward the pole of the horizon. Days are lengthening and the cold is strengthening, but there is a new spirit in the land. It is the heart of winter, but one can feel the increasing momentum as the days climb up the slope toward spring. Meadows and upland pastures are locked in sleep. The ice-covered brooks run sluggishly to their destinations. Snow banks are high along the roads, and the paths to the R.F.D. box and to the hen house are narrow canyons between steep sides. The lowland swamps are open to the sky; thin shadows run from naked trees on hardwood ridges. Gray-black smoke spirals up from farm chimneys and drifts away on the cold, clear air. Ax blows echo from wood lots, and sled runners squeak over hard-packed snow.

There is, however, a new spirit in the air in January. It is the time of seed catalogues and the making of plans. After a day of thaw, icicles hang from woodshed and barn in the morning. Those who live close to the land sense the added minutes of daylight. The telephone wires sing a song of increased tempo on bright days, and the evergreens murmur with excitement in the wind. It is winter, but the season has started uphill to spring.

SAUSAGE-MAKING TIME

AT the deepening edge of winter when steady cold has settled in and the hills and fields are white-covered with snow, a farmer makes plans for the butchering. After the meat is cut and trimmed, the hams and bacon prepared for the smoke-house, and the squares of fat sides readied for the big brine barrel beneath the cellar stairs, it's time to make sausage.

Sausage making is a process that keeps a young man around the kitchen. It's one day when the wood box is kept filled with pieces of dry, gray birch—a wood that gives a quick, hot fire. The old recipe, handed down through the generations, is easy to follow: three parts fresh lean meat, one part fat. A lad is glad to turn the grinder and watch the ground meat come pushing through the holes. The mechanical part is easy.

But when it comes to just the right amount of seasoning, advice is needed. The countryman is called in for his opinion. The only way to tell whether the sage, nutmeg, black pepper, and salt are in the right proportions is to fry a few cakes. Then the spicy, nostril-tickling aroma of the frying meat fills the kitchen and infiltrates through the back room and out into the ell. There's no fragrance quite like that of frying sausage. A man and a boy would solemnly eat their samples and look at each other. "I think," the countryman would say, "that it needs

146

just a little more sage and possibly a trifle more pepper. Sausage isn't sausage unless it's well spiced." That was the right answer, and a lad could spend a few minutes cutting kindling while the sausage was reworked, for in a short time a new sample would need to be tried. That was one of the satisfying things about making sausage; several samplings were required before it was ready to be stuffed into the cloth casing.

GRANITE STEPS

THERE is meaningful history in worn granite steps. For two centuries and more they have served their purpose. Some are the round, flat-topped granite stones at kitchen doors. Others have lain, little used, before the front doors that lead to the small formal parlors with their horsehair sofas and intricately carved whatnots. Big granite rocks have served as stepping stones to the doorsills of ells and woodsheds. One sees them slanting up to the big barn doorways and at the entrance to the tie-ups. Many an oldtime barn had a stairway made of steps for the cows to go up and down from the barn cellar. Far back on abandoned country roads that wind along hillsides and dip into hollows there are abandoned old cellar holes. The granite steps that led into these homes of yesteryear are appealing reminders of the days when children's voices echoed over open fields—fields long since reclaimed by Nature's forces.

These granite steps are the natural stones left on the land or in it by the slow-moving glaciers of long ago. One can imagine the work involved in bringing them to places where they would serve the needs of man: a pioneer driving a yoke or two of big, plodding oxen hitched to a stoneboat, the farm boys, the huge chains, and the heavy crossbars to help in their removal. When the clearings in the woodlands became fields and the log cabins had served their purpose, a man built a frame house for his family. Mothers and wives probably searched the fields and pastures in advance for the flat-topped rocks that would serve as doorsteps.

The era of the natural stone steps, before man learned to split granite for his needs, was an integral part of a new nation's development. Solid granite steps were part of the homes of long ago. On many farms they still serve. They have known the footsteps of past generations; they will know the footsteps of generations yet to come.

TEACHING A CALF TO DRINK

BABY calves are appealing creatures. A young man who likes livestock is willing to admit this fact. Their wobbly legs, big wondering eyes, and floppy ears give them a definite personality. On most farms after the little fellows have had the essential mothers' milk for a couple of days, it is common practice to teach them to drink skim milk from a bucket. That's a lad's job—and a battle that he has learned to enjoy.

Countrymen vary in their adherence to techniques. One group believes that mobile warfare is the logical approach. In the center of the pen one straddles the calf, puts the bucket of warm milk on the floor, dips a finger in the milk, inserts the finger in the baby bovine's oral cavity, and tries to push its head down to the milk. The calf will twist and turn and strug-

gle. Between trying to hold the youngster's head down, trying to keep the calf near the bucket, and trying to keep the bucket upright, one is certain to have a few lively minutes. Those who use this method claim it is best, however, because one has space in which to maneuver.

The other technique is one in which the issue may be consummated more quickly. Back the calf into a corner of the pen so its rear end is confined by the angle formed by the two sides. With the stern under control the bow is more amenable to reason. Then despite the inevitable struggle, the calf's head can be forced down to the milk. Both plans assume that the major objective is to convince the calf that by putting its mouth down instead of up, a pleasant result will occur. Of course, as many men know from experience, the calf will snort and blow in either case, and a boy will get generous splashes of milk on his overalls.

GRAY PHILOSOPHERS

YOU will see them on the hillsides, on upland fields, and along the winding back-country dirt roads. Sometimes they stand in groves, reminding one of the outdoor temples where the Druids gathered in days before man began to make a record of his history. The beeches with their huge trunks and spreading branches are the gray philosophers of the tree family. Through the decades they stand, benignly tolerant of the fevered foibles of man-made society.

The gray beech, *Fagus americana,* is a handsome, dignified tree. It has beauty throughout the year. The paper-textured, thin leaves hold their green sheen through the heat and drought of summer. At season's end the leaves turn shining gold. In spring the green-gold blossoms hang on pendulant stems. Many a man remembers the autumn days when he went to the beech grove to gather the triangular nuts that grow in the spiny cases. A century and more ago the wild pigeons fed on them, and pioneers let their hogs roam the woods in the fall to fatten on the sweet meats.

When white men first came to the new nation, there were huge forests of beeches. Mile on mile the big trees covered valleys and low mountains. Now the great stands of the trees are gone; they have played their role in the drama of a developing nation. The tough durable wood served pioneers for plank floors, for furniture, and for hand-hewed equipment. A goodly number of the trees remain. Alone or in groves they add beauty to the countryside. They stand through the years —an example of patience and beauty to men who too often forget to lift their eyes to the message that Nature is waiting to give.

INDIAN PUDDING

THE countryman does not wish to be considered persnickety about his food. But since one eats three times a day over a period of years, it seems logical to devote a reasonable amount of attention to the subject. Some do not realize that if a man takes nourishment three times a day for his allotted three score and ten, he consumes 76,650 meals. This figure, of course, is picayunish in terms of the astronomical numbers so carelessly flung about nowaday. Nevertheless if a man is going to eat more than 75,000 meals, it is only common sense to do a bit of planning about desserts.

The Indians gave us many things: among them, beans, potatoes, pumpkins, squashes, maple syrup, and maize. It was maize that helped the Pilgrims through the first bitter years. Today corn is the most important grain in our economy. With due credit to the satisfactions of beefsteaks and pork chops, johnnycake and brown bread, the most efficacious and delicious way yet devised to utilize corn meal is in Indian pudding. It is regrettable that so few know the quintessence of its epicurean savoriness in this form.

The ingredients are simple: 3 cups scalded whole milk, 1 cup light cream, 2½ tablespoons butter, ½ cup molasses, ½ cup maple syrup, 1 teaspoon salt, ⅔ teaspoon cinnamon, ½ teaspoon ginger, 2 eggs, 1¼ cups cold creamy milk, 5 tablespoons yellow corn meal. Cook in a moderate oven for about 3 hours. Don't go artistic and put in nuts or raisins. And *don't* smear whipped cream on it. There's only one way to serve Indian pudding. When a cereal dishful of the fragrant, nostril-tickling goodness is placed in front of you, pour on a generous amount of rich cream. Two helpings of the hot delicious pudding and a couple of glasses of cold milk are a most acceptable ending to a winter's day.

PATIENCE OF WINTER

MAN constantly evolves new instruments of power and increases his tempo of living. But Earth is infinitely patient, and the cycling seasons follow their appointed rounds with unhurried regularity. Man gropes toward the ultimate sources of power and learns to speed himself and his products around the planet. Nature ordains the time of sowing and the time of reaping. In each cycle of time while Earth follows her course around the sun, there is a period of rest.

He who will, can learn a lesson in living from the patience of winter. The snowstorm that disrupts man's taut order of business means deeper, safer covering for the roots of trees and grasses. Meadows and upland fields sleep beneath protective cover. Valley creeks and pasture brooks make muted music as slow water flows toward the deepness of the sea. Swamps that are places of murky mystery in the lushness of summer lie open and exposed, patiently waiting through the months of gray quietness.

You can feel winter's patience in the sugar bush where gaunt, rough-barked maples stand guard around weathered saphouses. You can feel the quiet acceptance of winter in the groves of white pines and hemlocks. You can hear it in the subdued murmuring of the branches overhead. Walk along a country road and you can see Earth's patience in the scraggly arms of the sumacs lifted above snow-capped stone walls. Climb to a pasture hilltop on a January day and look across the sleeping valley to the windrows of mountains against the horizon. Winter is the time of patience, and in the season's lesson is meaning for him who is attuned to the verities of life.

EARTH revolves on her axis and travels her path around the sun. Bodies of matter millions of miles distant wheel into line twice a year, and the seasons follow each other with unvarying regularity. The uplift of spring levels into the lushness of summer. And when Nature's time of replenishment is fulfilled, autumn's banners proclaim the time of thanksgiving for another harvest. Winter is the period of low tension, and in the land's frozen top layer roots and bulbs go through the mysterious and profound changes that ready them for the miracle of rebirth.

Winters follow a general pattern, but once in a decade, once in a generation, or once in a century the unpredictable forces of air currents, temperature, and moisture combine to send snow of memorable depth. Then if the snow be light and the wind forceful, there is a time of deep drifts. On cold, sunny days when the red line hovers near zero, snow whirls in circling, twisting lines over level meadows and sloping fields. Lines of dry loose particles whish back and forth on pasture hillsides and play in changing formations in the orchard.

Deep drifts grow deeper in the ravines by the woods and pile against the sides of barns, corncribs, and houses. The heaps of snow fill the hollows at lower ends of mowings and make sculptured patterns above granite boulders and in field corners. Smoothly carved, overhanging masses outline the banks of meadow creeks and northland rivers and form spaced windrows on pasture sides where the cow tracks have been worn into the soil. Deep drifts cause extra labor in man's taut order, but it is a time of poignant beauty on the countryside.

FRIDAY afternoon exercises in the district school were an important aspect of the winter social season. Winter was the period when life on the farm slowed down. There was always enough to do, to be sure; but the press of living lightened, and the grownups enjoyed going to the Friday afternoon exercises.

By unwritten agreement, the members of the school committee and the farm families gave teacher the autumn weeks to get started. By January things had shaken down, and teacher would have been disappointed if visitors had not shown up at three o'clock to see and applaud the hour's program.

In retrospect, there is something typically American, typically democratic, about the programs that were given in one- and two-room schools. From one to three on Fridays came the final rehearsing of the program. The big boys who were not taking part had a comfortable working agreement with teacher. If they didn't make any noise, their lessons would be skipped in return for washing the blackboards, dusting the erasers, sweeping the floor and the front entry, cleaning up around the stove, and rearranging the pile of wood in the corner. That was a good example of practical democracy.

The program itself was always interesting. There were group songs, duets, and solos; there were pieces spoken by little tots and occasionally by a big eighth-grader who enjoyed his reputation as an orator. "Up from the meadows, rich with corn" and "Hew down the bridge, Sir Consul" have echoed in schoolhouses across the land. Tense mothers, with babies on their laps, moved their lips in unison with their six-, seven-, and eight-year-olds who recited pieces the mothers and fathers

156

knew better than their children. Sometimes the chairman of the school committee gave the words for the spelling match. Perhaps a farmer, who had graduated from the local academy, asked some expected, standard geography questions. Many a man looking back to those Friday afternoon exercises, knows he learned much from them never gained from books.

SATURDAY NIGHT BATH

IT is time to say something about Saturday night baths. As one reads about the imaginative marvels to come it is interesting to note that taking a bath will be made easy and very pleasant. In fact, if the dreamers have their way, it will be nearly automatic. As soon as one steps into the shower stall, an electric eye will turn on the water at just the right temperature. Soap will be mixed with the water, so one will not have to grope desperately for an elusive, slippery cake of congealed grease. And when the water has done its duty, warm, drying air will circulate like a midsummer breeze. No longer will there be a moist spot in the center of one's back.

A generation ago taking the weekly bath was a major process. A lad, however recalcitrant, knew it was inevitable. On a cold midwinter night it seemed unnecessary labor. It was not like a hot summer afternoon when one had put in hours of sweaty, grimy work haying or cultivating corn. Then it was logical to take a bath. Besides, it was fun to dive into the cool, dark water of the swimming pool in the creek.

The Saturday night bath in the farm kitchen in winter was vastly different. The water had to be heated in kettles and pans on the top of the big kitchen stove. The tin tub—the same one in which the clothes were washed—was placed in front of the stove. Water was precious, and about four inches was the accepted depth. There were two methods, neither satisfactory to a boy. He could stand up and by reaching down, get water and toss it over himself. This was the quicker method but not favored by Mother, who was always skeptical of complete coverage. The other method was to sit in the tub with his knees under his chin and the edge of the tub cutting a crease in his back just above the fourth vertebra. Both methods resulted in plenty of splashes on the floor.

Saturday night baths have a definite place in our nation's history, but many lads have felt the custom of bathing once a week in winter was greatly overrated.

BOX SUPPER

THERE are a number of things this country needs; some of them are imperative. In the latter category the countryman places a revival of box suppers. A generation ago these affairs were high lights of the social season. Box suppers have not gone over the hill to join bustles and beards as outmoded institutions, but these old-fashioned, jolly get-togethers are now infrequent and puny in their influence.

Time was when a box supper was a Brobdingnagian affair. On the surface, of course, everything was kept to the routine pattern. Some worthy organization like the Grange, the Ladies' Aid Society, or the Village Athletic Association needed a lift in its finances. Even Barnum could not improve on the rural scheme of getting something for nothing and selling it at a good price. This is the skeleton of a box supper. All the girls bring boxes of food. The town auctioneer, quick of wit and glib of tongue, gives his services. The highest bidder gets the box—and the lady who prepared it as his supper partner.

Now there are areas of common sense. The married folks who have known each other for years and have responsibilities acknowledge an unwritten agreement that a dollar is about enough for a box. Such a price helps the cause along and does not hurt the pocketbook. Then there are the teen-age fry who want certain boxes. They can go to two or three dollars—and do, with lots of shouting and egging on by the auctioneer who knows the reason why certain boxes are well up the scale. The climax comes when two young bachelors are after the new school teacher's offering. The competition is one part of the fun of a box supper. The other is the good neighborliness and fellowship that come when people take time off from the chores of daily living to get together and break bread.

FIXING FOR A STORM

COUNTRYMEN respect the gadgets and wavy-lined graphs of scientists who plot the complicated weather maps. Farmers conscientiously read the reports in the paper and listen to the voices on the wireless, although they wish the prognosticators would dispense with so many qualifying statements. A man who has lived on the land for half a century does not need to hedge with reputation-saving phrases. He knows for certain it is fixing for a storm.

For two days there has been a blue sky with a gun-metal gray haze along the western horizon. For two nights the stars have been bright. The haze around the waxing moon has been thicker over the top segment than below it. For two evenings a breeze has freshened at dusk and then died away by the time the countryman went out for his nine o'clock look at the livestock.

Now in the third morning, gray clouds are climbing from the northeast. Winter silence is on the meadows, mowings, and uplands. Up and down the valley road the smoke from farmhouse chimneys spirals high and then drifts slowly away toward the southwest. Through forenoon hours the quietness deepens. The thin sound of chopping comes from a neighbor's wood lot. The spaced, sweet tones of the village bell float slowly by. The poignant whistle of the train in the valley carries clearly as the long-drawn-out lonesome wail echoes from the upland heights. Hour by hour the silence thickens; hour by hour the gray shade on the countryside deepens. At noon, when he comes in from feeding the horses, the countryman stands for a minute by the ell door. Hushed expectancy broods over the Earth. It is fixing for a storm.

FRIED POTATOES

IN a land where men have been known to sprinkle sugar on baked beans, it is not surprising to learn that there are differences of opinion about fried potatoes. Still, it is difficult to reconcile the intransigency of the minority regarding the fundamentals of such an important dish.

160

By and large, countrymen agree that the best fried potatoes are made from new potatoes. A farmer usually plants a couple of rows very early in the year. If a frosty night occurs, it is only a matter of a few minutes to pull soft soil over the young plants. By the middle of September the new potatoes are at their best. There is nothing wrong with boiled potatoes, milk gravy, and fried salt pork for a noon meal when a man comes in from the field, but it is the fried potatoes he has for supper that really hit the spot.

The best fried potatoes are made in an iron spider on a wood-burning stove. After a few slices of bacon have been fried crisp and broken into small pieces and the surplus fat drained off, the cold, previously boiled potatoes are sliced into the sizzling pan. Then the housewife moves the spider back a bit on the stove, puts on a cover, and forgets it while the contents heat through. About the time a farmer is stripping the last cow, she takes off a front cover and puts the spider directly over the heat. In a few minutes the slices are brown and crisp. No matter if some of the small pieces are hard and crunchy. That is all to the good.

As a man comes in from his chores, he smells that rich, satisfying fragrance before he gets to the kitchen. Fried potatoes with a few pieces of yellow corn-meal bread, plenty of grape jelly and sweet chutney, plus applesauce, chocolate cake, and two glasses of rich, cold milk make an excellent supper.

FEBRUARY'S MESSAGE

WHEN February's sun sends sharper angled rays to white-blanketed hills and fields, there's a mellowness on quiet sunny days that foretells the closing era of winter. The second month has much in common with the eleventh. The first part of November clings to a remembrance of autumn and the latter half hints a warning of ominous cold. February reverses the messages. The first half of the month strives to sink its grappling irons into the solidness of winter's heart; the second half proves that the anchors are slipping.

It is the time of year when sleeping Earth stirs with the first restlessness of a new season. Zero spells and blustery snow and sleet make treacherous footing. But each time the cold relaxes its grip and each time the storm-spilling, dark nimbus clouds break away to blue skies and white cumulus masses, the new season takes a firmer grip and hitches itself upward toward spring.

Walk over the land on a pleasant day and you can read the messages of the new season in the swelling buds of red maples in the swamps and in the plump kittens of pussy willows along the meadow creek. You can see it in the cringing, grainy snow of mowing fields and in the bare spots on the south side of the wood lot. You can smell it in the resinous fragrance of the pines and spruces; you can hear it in the melodious bugling of the blue jays and in the staccato snaps of shrinking ice along the pasture brook. Day by day the hours of light grow longer and sunset's glory lingers in the sky above the mountain's rim.

In the evening Mars and Saturn make a nest of brightness with Castor and Pollux. February can be contradictory, but each day the calendar chips off a sliver of shrinking winter.

DRIED APPLE PIES

WHEN the season has pulled itself along into February and the weathered icehouse is filled with sawdust-packed, green-white cakes from the village pond, the countryman begins to hanker for dried apple pies. The second month, due to Octavius's contrivings, is the shortest of them all. But its back-and-forth weather stretches the days on a long sagging string. Correctly made dried apple pies help one along to the time of March promise.

People used to take the situation with the seriousness it deserves. In October the apple parer was fastened to the table on the porch, and the family spent a day getting the fruit ready. After the apples, preferably Baldwins, Limbertwigs, and Maiden Blush, were pared, quartered, cored, and sliced, the pieces were strung on linen threads and hung to dry in the sun. The rich, tangy fragrance spread through the ell, woodshed, and kitchen. When the slices were dried sufficiently, the wizened curled pieces were stored in brown paper bags in the attic.

There's nothing complicated about making a dried apple pie, but it must be done according to rule. The slices must be soaked in water for several hours. They should be mixed with raisins and a few pieces of lemon peel for added tartness, seasoned with a whiffle of salt, and sweetened with a small spoon-

ful of molasses. Any pie, of course, to rate any merit must be close to an inch in thickness. A generous wedge or two of dried apple pie, covered with thick yellow cream and topped with a light sprinkling of maple sugar, is one way to start a pleasant evening before the kitchen stove with the seed catalogues.

RED-AND-WHITE CHECKED TABLE CLOTH

THE farm kitchen used to be the family gathering place, and the big table with its red-and-white checked cloth served many purposes. While Mother and sisters cleared the table after the five o'clock supper, washed the dishes, and redded up, Father and the boys did the milking and separating, and bedded down the stock for the night. By six-thirty or so, the family was ready for its pleasant evening routine.

The young folks sat around the table. Books and homework were scattered on the cloth; the Lazy Susan was pushed to one end, and the big-bowled kerosene lamp with its creamy-white shade resting on brass arms was placed in the center. Spelling, geography, and arithmetic lessons had to be studied and papers prepared for the next day. Usually a lad had a mail-order catalogue by his elbow; perhaps he also had a copy of *Hunting and Trapping in the North Woods.* When a fellow was exhausted from studying such words as "incompatibility" and "Popocatepetl" and the examples in long division grew unconscionably stubborn, he needed a few moments of relaxation to recover momentum.

The red-and-white checked cloth was used for other pur-

poses. Here on a stormy winter afternoon Father wrote out
the annual list from the seed catalogue. He ordered the main-
crop seeds while Mother took care of the list for the kitchen
garden, and the petunias, asters, snapdragons, zinnias, and
calendulas for her flower garden. Each fall and spring the family sat around the table and compiled the list to go to the mail-
order house. And when the young folks grew up and left the
farms in search of adventure, Mothers sat at the big tables to
write letters to them in far-off places. The red-and-white
checked spreads have been familiar props on the home stage
as the drama of a growing nation has unfolded.

SNOW TREES

TWO or three times a winter the clouds drop deep blankets of
heavy moist snow. In that period after January's strength has
diminished and before the ground hog has poked from his
burrow to decide whether or not he should curl up again for
a six weeks' snooze, there is often an interlude when the
Weather Man drops a clinging snow. One can almost smell
the storm approaching as the gathering stratus and cirrus
clouds stitch a gray canvas over the pale blue sky. They quickly
condense to black-streaked nimbus clouds, and in a matter of
hours the large sticky flakes begin to drop on the waiting land.

There's something restful about this type of winter storm.
All earth is quiet and patient. The winds are hitched in their
stables. The big fluffy snow stars seem to wander casually down
through the soft gray light. The winter wildlife of woodland,
meadow, and hedgerow has sought protection in burrows and

beneath the branches of evergreens. Through dim daylight hours and the still blackness of night, the flakes fall silently and steadily.

In the early hours of a new day when the clouds have disappeared and the sun shines from a clear sky, the snow trees make a fairyland of beauty. All of Earth's trees and shrubs wear cloaks of white. The maples, oaks, and elms are gray and white etchings in the bright sunlight. The spruces, hemlocks, firs, and white pines are draped in white and green, their branches bent low, making obeisance to the Storm King. For a few breath-taking hours there's loveliness on the land. It is Nature's winter ball when the trees put on their beautiful gowns for a formal party.

WINTER SWAMP

THOREAU was partial to swamps. "When I would recreate myself," he wrote, "I seek the darkest wood, the thickest and most interminable and, to the citizen, most dismal swamp. I enter a swamp as a sacred place. There is the strength, the marrow of Nature. The wild-wood covers the virgin-mold, and the same soil is good for men and trees. A township where one primitive forest waves above while another primitive forest rots below—such a town is fitted to raise not only corn and potatoes, but poets and philosophers for the coming ages."

When Time has climbed over the hump of winter and a rain followed by a quick weather change has given the snow a hard crust for ease of walking, it's a good time to go into the heart of a swamp. The black-water pools are covered with ice.

The muskrats' huts are white domes dotted among the hummocks; they wear etchinglike plumes of frost-bleached swamp grass. Raggedy fluffs of last season's cylindrical blossoms cap the sturdy cattail stems. Bulky, loose squirrels' nests are stark blotches in the red maples.

The chestnut red of the high-bush blueberry buds throws a glint of color in the scraggly, thick-growing clumps. White birches in their virgin robes hold drooping arms to the climbing sun. Soft, filtered light lays a pewter-gray pattern on the floor of the evergreen groves. There's a clean, bracing aroma from the spruces, firs, and hemlocks. Listen carefully and you will hear a murmuring among the branches overhead—a soft conversation that says the trees are waiting patiently for the miracle of rebirth that is on the way. If there is a light snow over the crust, one can read the stories written by pheasants, wood mice, rabbits, and perhaps a fox on their daily rounds.

Once a year in winter a man should go into a swamp. He can feel the power that has locked Earth's breast. The mystery of summer lies revealed in the clear light of Nature's sleeping time.

THAWING OUT THE PUMP

A YOUNG man realized that certain jobs were part of his work on the farm. He couldn't expect to get out of turning the grindstone; in season he expected to weed the strawberries and thin the carrots. But on a winter's morning when the red line in the thermometer was below the zero mark, he wished that thawing out the barnyard pump was not a regular chore.

Sometimes, of course, the pump at the kitchen sink caught, but that pump was usually open to reason and quickly responded to a dipperful of hot water.

The barnyard pump was a stubborn affair although long experience had taught him the technique of thawing it out. No use trying to hurry things. Inanimate objects can display an unconscionable amount of patience-testing perversity. Before a boy went out to help with the morning milking, he put two copper kettles over the front covers of the stove and stoked the firebox with oak and maple. After breakfast he took the boiling water and went to work. Too bad the man who wrote the ad in the catalogue didn't have to thaw out what he called the "new pattern, close-top, antifreeze lift pump" himself.

One went at it carefully. Just a bit of the hot water. Work the creaking handle up and down. A little more water. Work the handle steadily. Not too fast. More water. Still that raucous, hollow, gawking noise. More water. More handle pumping. Pour water with one hand; work the handle with the other. Second tea kettle almost gone. Would the water come? Suddenly a welcome sound. A deeper, purposeful gurgle. More hot water. The feel of weight as water started. Then one could relax. He could feel the water on the way up before the cold, crackling liquid splashed into the trough.

Thawing out the pump is still a morning chore on northland farms. A lad doesn't pretend to understand atomic fission, but when the new power is under control, he hopes some of it will be hitched to pumps beside the farm watering troughs.

THERE are a number of reasons why the world in general is in a fretting, irritable mood. People want too much for too little; they don't eat enough at breakfast; there are too few three-layer chocolate cakes; and the ladies use too much parsley on plain foods. . . . But one of the major reasons for the jittery, riled waters of the social, cultural, and economic mill ponds is that men no longer whittle when they have a problem to discuss.

There was a time when whittling was a recognized and essential part of the scene Americana. A man was not properly equipped for the day's living without a good jackknife. On stormy days in winter countrymen relaxed in the comfortable farm shops with a piece of pine and a good knife. When they went to the blacksmith shop or to the feed store in town, they expected to sit on boxes and old chairs and do a bit of whittling.

Whittling is more than a casual way of passing a few leisurely minutes. Good countrymen know that it is at once an expression of creative art and a help to a man who is trying to develop a logical philosophy in an illogical world. It requires a razor-keen blade, a piece of clear-grained wood, and an objective. On the farm there are always plenty of the latter: new teeth for the long-handled wooden rake, a new tooth for the bull rake, slender but strong oaken or maple pegs for the harness room, a sharp-angled hook from which to hang the lanterns behind the tie-up.

Whittling is more than an occupation for men's fingers. As a man slowly and carefully fashions the article, his mind is free to ponder life's strangeness and idiosyncrasies. He wishes that when men get together in congressional halls and international conclaves, they would pull out knives and pieces of wood and start whittling. Men who whittle usually arrive at logical compromises.

SHOVEL SLIDING

ALONG in February when the Weather Man sent a thaw and one could almost feel Earth relax from winter tautness, a young man looked forward to a spell of good sliding. It was fun to coast down hill roads after the snow roller had packed the going smooth. On long hills with deep thank-you-ma'ams and a curve or two it was reasonably exciting. But the best fun came when a cold spell followed a thaw or a warm rain. Then the fields and slopes were ice-hard. One could start at the top of the upland pasture, shoot down through the roadside barway, and rush far over the meadow on a lightweight double runner.

It wasn't a real winter, however, unless a lad had a chance to do some shovel sliding. There was nothing quite like it in the realm of transportation. The big steel sawdust scoop that one used to bed down the cows at night made a perfect sled. The steep slope that slanted upward from the pasture ravine was a made-to-order spot. One settled one's posterior firmly in the scoop, held the handle in one's hands, and took off. The crust was as slippery as ice, and in a few yards one had gathered exciting momentum. The shovel took unpredictable swoops, swirls, and side tangents. Sometimes the unevenness of a hummock would throw one into a spin and a dozen neck-snapping circles. On a zeroish day tears streamed from wind-burned eyes, and a fellow lay back a moment on the crust over the brook to catch his breath.

Modern folks prefer swooping over soft snow on waxed wooden slats, but the countryman still claims shovel sliding is the best of winter sports.

BARN DOORWAYS

THERE'S something about a barn doorway that sets it apart from other places on the farm. It's away from the house, for one thing, and a countryman doesn't have to think about the dirt and mud on his boots. It's a big and spacious opening, and a man likes a place to sit and rest himself where there's plenty of room all around. On thawing days toward the end of winter, when the water runs from the roof and little rivulets come around the end of the barn and move across the sloping yard to the road, when the February sun courses across a blue sky and the crows are poking around in the stubble, it's good to "set" for a spell after the midday meal in the barn doorway.

Naturally, the door should be on the south side of the barn so a man can absorb the warming rays of Helios's chariot. There should be a couple of old boxes around or perhaps an upended nail keg. Some countrymen, who have learned that resting comfortably is one of the more important arts of living, have picked up an old chair or two to keep in the barn. Somehow the big open space is the center of farm activity. Through the doors in summer go the great heaped loads of hay. On a sunny day in late winter the hens like to scratch there in the chaff and hayseed. The farm collie chooses the barn doorway for his after-dinner nap.

With his back against the door jamb, the countryman enjoys the spot for his noon interlude. There's a sense of security and peace. It's good to smell the pungent aroma from the stable, the dry, tangy fragrance of the hay on the scaffolds, that satisfying blend of smells that comes from a barn on a sunny day. One can hear the rattle of the chains as the cows reach for the last wisps of hay and the stamping of the horses in their stalls. In the hen house a biddy proclaims that she has laid an egg.

Barn doorways were built primarily for a utilitarian purpose. But a man knows that in nice weather they also provide a good place to sit and think—or just to sit.

SNOWDRIFTS IN THE SKY

THERE are winter days when clouds are piled like snowdrifts in a blue sky. Winter's wardrobe is chiefly a symphony of gray hues. Meadow grasses are gray-brown above the snow; alders and willows are gray-border stitching along the gray-ice ribbons of creeks. Thin gray shadows run from the trunks of maples and oaks on the upland ridges, and stone walls are gray chains along the roads and around the mowings.

There come days when a brassy sun pulls up from the mountain rim into an ultramarine sky. The slanting rays have a peculiar brilliance and distant details are starkly clear. After an hour or two pure-white cumulus clouds begin drifting upward from the sharply silhouetted jagged line of the mountain top. Soon snowdrifts are piled all over the sky.

174

They are not the huge rounded masses of clouds that one sees in June or in September. These are smaller in size and elongated in shape. Slowly they climb from the horizon and make a pattern against the blue until the whole heaven is covered with the drifts.

For an hour or two at midday they make a beautiful picture. The countryman pauses at his wood chopping to look through the branches of the trees. He knows that the alternate lines of blue and white are a weather sign. The cloud cycle follows a definite course: from cumulus to cirrus, cirrus to nimbus—and the nimbus means snow. For a brief interlude there is beauty overhead as clouds form snowdrifts in the sky.

BUGGY WHIPS

A MAN does not want to be unreasonable, but there's one thing about which he holds definite conclusions. If he has a horse and uses it to drive to town, he is entitled to a buggy whip of his own choice. The womenfolks, of course, are prone to have opinions about anything that involves flair and color. Sisters of a certain age are much concerned with pastel shades and feel that the artistic path is the right approach to life's quandaries. But the choice of a buggy whip rightly belongs to the menfolks.

The purchase of a new whip was a matter of major moment in a farm family. A farmer didn't pretend it was essential; a young man wouldn't dream of using it on the friendly, lively Morgans. But the fact was that neither a buggy nor a stylish sleigh was completely equipped without a whip of color and distinction. Therefore, when Father announced one evening after supper that it might be a good idea to see what the mail-order catalogues were offering this season, a lad was prompt and possibly a bit officious with his sisters as he pored over the advertisements of equine equipment.

The names themselves made satisfying reading: "Hindoo Rawhide, Magic Wire Woven, Gladstone Buggy, Gray Fox Rawhide, Knickerbocker Nickel Ferrule, and Spanish Rose." With a foundation of such good mouth-filling designations, one read proudly and eagerly the description of the final choice. "Dolly Varden rawhide center, reinforced vellum tanned rawhide loop, handworked buttons, scarlet-red braided handsome tassel of genuine, imported first-quality silk, light-loaded butt which gives good swinging effect. A stylish combination of red, black, blue, and orange." When a man had pride in his sleekly groomed horse, his painted buggy or sleigh with red striping, and his harness freshly oiled and glistening, an eye-arresting, colorful whip was the essential item to complete his equipage.

LITTLE CARPENTER

ANY day now there will be a resonant staccato drum roll from the old Baldwin behind the barn or from the gaunt, scraggly August Sweet at the corner of the icehouse. It will likely be a mellow blue-sky day when tumbled masses of white cumulus clouds foretell the nearness of March and drops of water from icicles play a muffled tick-tack on the cement apron before the open barn doors. The little carpenter's drumming is a harbinger of spring.

Although the downy woodpecker is the most common member of his family, he is brimming with personality and individuality. He's a perky little troubadour in his cloak of black and white with a red cap set at a jaunty angle on the back of his head. His demure mate is also dressed in black and white but has no scarlet headgear. The bitterness of winter holds no terror for the downy; he lives up to his imposing name: *Dryobates pubescens.* In November or early December he drills a snug shelter hole in a decaying trunk or limb of a tree.

The carpenter birds are almost as particular as the bluebirds about selecting a home. Through March and into April they spend hours exploring trees. They poke around fussily, talking back and forth in metallic, nasal chirps. In and out of a knot hole they fly, checking and double-checking. *Dryobates* is one of the few birds who prepares the nest for his mate. Actually it's not much of a home since the five or six tiny white eggs are laid on bare wood at the bottom of the cavity.

Through the winter months the downies come to the window sill feeder. As they cling to the edge, one can see their unusual foot structure: two toes in front and two in back instead of the usual three in front and one behind. Their spiny tail feathers serve as an anchor against the tree trunks. Their long horny-tipped tongues are efficient spears for insects, grubs, and larvae.

The little carpenter is a philosopher; he takes the weather as it comes. But one of these days his drumming will be heard, and the countryman will know that the downy is forecasting the new season.

MARCH PROMISE

TWICE each year it happens. Somewhere in those great spaces that astronomers discuss in terms of millions of miles the planets and stars wheel into line. There's a brief item in the newspaper that for another fleeting instant in the billion-year panorama of Earth's history, day and night are equal in length. Countrymen who live close to Nature's moods look across fields and hills and wonder if an equinoctial storm is on the way.

March is a symphony whose music runs the whole gamut. Within its thirty-one days one usually hears the low, hushed movement that pays tribute to winter's power when Earth's breast is hard and her pulse is faint and slow. There's a crescendo movement when the warm winds creep up from the southland and begin pulling at the stitches that hold life in bounds. Toward the end of the month, after the equinox, the tempo rises, and the cymbals and drums crash out the news to a stirring world that spring has at last arrived.

Trickling waters course down the sidehill mowings and the pasture slopes. Pussy willows lift their gray-furred blooms along winding creeks; the first yellow tinge of opening forsythias makes color by the garden wall. Blue jays bugle as they flash through the sugar grove, and one happy day the bluebirds arrive in the orchard behind the barn and throw plaintive arias to the sky. White masses of cumulus clouds move across the blue field overhead. Earth shakes itself from winter's drowsiness, and the sap flows upward to swelling buds. Men raise their heads, and their hearts quicken to the surgings of the great miracle. March is the month of promise—the promise that after the time of cold and snow a new season is at hand.

HORSE SHEDS

POETS have sung the praises of the white-spired churches that face green village commons and busy town squares. The white clapboard town halls of rural hamlets have had their share of attention. But sparse has been the notice paid to the horse sheds behind the churches and the civic centers.

Sometimes the stalls were built in a straight row, other times in a semicircle. Today they may stand empty and silent; or perhaps they store some of the town's road-working machinery, big scrapers or drags, or a pile of planks drying out to replace worn sections of the weathered bridges that span placid creeks or tumbling brooks.

There was a time, however, when the horse sheds were an integral part of rural life. On Sunday mornings when farm families came to worship in the village church, the horses were hitched in the sheds. In winter when snow blanketed the hills and the valleys, there would be a row of pungs, cutters, and sleighs. Sometimes when a family had six or eight children, one saw a big two-horse sled with high board sides. On a blanket-covered layer of straw and with buffalo robes around them, large families of youngsters could be transported comfortably. On a Sunday morning in summer the row would consist of sturdy two-seated democrats, one-seated buggies, fringed-topped surreys, and perhaps a canopied carryall.

180

On town-meeting day in March, the shed behind the town hall was always full. Throughout the year both lines of sheds were used as needed. On the boards above the stalls, pigeons and phoebes built their nests. Rats and mice cleaned up the grain spilled from the horses' canvas nose bags. There was dried hay on the earthen floor and deep holes where impatient horses pawed and stamped.

Gone is the use for which the horse sheds were intended. But still they stand in many villages—a reminder of the days when life moved pleasantly and leisurely.

PRUNING TIME

ON a sunny late-winter day when a gentle wind brings the first whisper of quickening spring, it's time to get out the ladder, the saw, and the hand clippers and to start pruning the apple trees. There's something satisfying about the work. For one thing, it isn't a rush job. At this time of year a farmer can work along leisurely. All too soon it will be sugaring season, and good sap weather means hustling day and night.

Apple orchards, of course, should be on a sidehill. If a man sets his ladder on the low side, he can look up to the sugar grove and the granite-ledged hill above. Working on the up side, there's a view of the fields and meadows in the valley and the blue-green mountains in the distance beyond the river.

Pruning a Baldwin, Northern Spy, or McIntosh requires both judgment and skill. A man has to study his tree. Too many limbs mean dense foliage, lack of sunlight, and poorly colored apples. The countryman is proud of his well-shaped,

181

widely branching trees. Pruning wisely takes a lot of unhurried study. It's a craftsman's job—with flush cuts and the removal of the right suckers and side branches.

Pruning apple trees on a pre-spring day, however, is more than sawing and clipping. It's a chance to see the countryside before it is unlocked. It gives a man an opportunity to study patterns in bark and to discover where the flickers have built their nests. He can hear a dog bark across the valley, and a cow rumbles a melancholy call from the farm down the road. Late in the afternoon when the brush has been piled up, his handiwork is clearly etched against the sky. As a farmer tramps down to the barn to do the evening chores, he rejoices that it's the season for pruning the apple trees.

THE ELL

CITY folks discourse on the quaintness of what they technically label "continuous architecture." Maybe an old-fashioned ell that connects a man's dwelling to his barn deserves some such flossy terminology, but the countryman doesn't bother much about it. As far as he is concerned, the ell is just one more illustration of the perspicacity of his pioneer ancestors who took a calculating look at the environment and built accordingly.

An ell is a man's fortress against the weather. On a zeroish morning after a snowstorm, or in the pelting rains of spring and autumn, it gives a man a certain snug sense of satisfaction to light his lantern, take the milk pails, and go along the familiar route through the back kitchen, woodshed, carriage shed, shop, grain room, and into the barn proper.

182

Ells are not hard and fast propositions. Some are short and chunky; others are long and narrow. Farmers of yesteryear were individualists, and they built their farmstead buildings to suit their own ideas. Two common denominators of all farms were the summer kitchen and the woodshed. The summer kitchen often had a big iron kettle in a brick arch and a large buttery in one corner. A spacious woodshed was essential. An ell gave a farmer a chance to have his carriages, sleighs, and farm shop in convenient juxtaposition to the yard. In a winter when snows fell deep and often, it was good to have one's chore work all under cover. Contrary to the occasional snide remarks of farmers out in the wild regions beyond the Alleghenies, this business of walking from the kitchen to the tie-up under a roof is not an illustration of New England conservatism or lack of pioneering qualities. An ell is a tangible example of plain, downright intelligence.

OLD SAPHOUSE

NO one has proposed a nationwide rehabilitation program for the dilapidated, weather-beaten, sagging-roofed saphouses that one finds in the sugar-maple groves. In Pennsylvania and Ohio, in Wisconsin and Michigan, in New York and New England, the saphouses are appealingly similar. They nestle close to the ground. Around them are the big, friendly rough-barked trees.

When the time of frosty, starry nights and warm, mellow days arrives, the old saphouse becomes the center of attention. If the Weather Man is kind and sends a succession of good days, the fires beneath the long evaporator pans are kept stoked day and night. Clouds of grayish steam rise from the bubbling liquid and swirl upward among the rafters.

Sapping time is a period of hard work. Struggling through softening snow, carrying pails of sap to the barrel on the sled, watching the fire at night—all these tasks spell labor. But there's always a sugaring off to bolster a lad's morale when the sap is running fast and work piles up. A party in the grove is the high light of the season. There is good fun on a crisp evening when friends and neighbors gather around the saphouse to eat the golden brown confection after it has been cooled on snow. Or perhaps one prefers to stir a saucerful of the heavy syrup until it becomes soft, creamy sugar. Of course, a lad sometimes needs to resort to pickles. There's nothing equal to a sour pickle to revive gustatory appreciation.

Then one mild day the farmer knows that the season is over. Buds are swelling and the sap is losing its sweetness. The equipment is gathered, cleaned, and stored away. The old saphouse is through for another season.

UPSIDE-DOWN FELLOW

HE'S a friendly, industrious bird whose New-Englandish nasal "ank-ank-ank" sounds during late winter days from the scraggly Red Astrachan trees behind the house. The white-breasted nuthatch does not deserve his cumbersome scientific title: *Sitta carolinensis carolinensis.* He likes to come around the farm buildings while a man is splitting wood and wheeling it to the shed. He's a topsy-turvy chap who prefers to go through life upside down. No other bird is in the same class when it comes to going headfirst down a tree trunk.

The whitebreast is a handsome fellow in a subdued, conservative way. His cap is a deep bluish black; his cloak is a rich blue gray; his waistcoat is a creamy white. His body is a little larger than a song sparrow's, but his short, squarish tail with white, black-tipped feathers seems to throw him out of proportion. It is interesting to watch a whitebreast proceed down-trunk in a vertical plane; one foot reaches forward under his breast while the other clings to the bark back under his tail.

All winter long the cheerful fellows come to the feeders. They are forehanded in attitude and often hide seeds and nuts under shingles, in crevices, and beneath bark. Come spring they withdraw from the farmstead and set up housekeeping in a tree cavity.

When the worst of winter is over, the upside-down birds give a daily show around the yard. Up and down the trunks they go. Once in a while one bird stops to hammer at a kernel wedged in a crack. It is this habit that gives the bird its every-day name. The whitebreasts don't rate highly as musicians; they are just a common year-round bird. But their steady talking and optimistic attitude make them welcome companions as winter's time runs out.

CORN BREAD AND—

THERE's a place in the nutritional field for such foods as thick T-bone steaks, juicy sirloin roasts a little on the rare side, flavorful pot roasts with plenty of delicious gravy intersticed with bits of carrots and onions, and lots of butter to spread on hot meats and mashed potatoes—all these have a place as long as corn bread is available.

185

We may as well face facts frankly. There are some persons who hold that beaten soda biscuits are superior to maize-based products. But to anyone who is sensitive to the delicate, almost intangible nuances of flavor, nothing quite equals corn bread. When a generous-sized pan of it comes hot and fragrant from the oven, a man knows he has a happy few minutes ahead. It should have a crisp, golden brown top. The corner pieces are especially desirable because then one gets top and two sides of brown crunchiness.

There are those who complain, albeit mildly as a rule, that corn bread is too crumbly; they cannot take a piece in hand without disintegration of the yellow deliciousness. Ah, but such people do not appreciate the full potentialities of the situation. Corn bread is meant to be consumed in alliance with other things. Some hold that ham gravy is the fitting partner; others stoutly insist that a generous amount of molasses is the only reasonable concomitant. We have been told that in the Northern States they use maple syrup. The point is: corn bread is at its best with a meat liquid. A man can use his fingers, his spoon, or a fork. Fingers will get sticky but that's a picayunish price to pay for a feed of corn bread—and meat gravy.

SUGAR SNOW

AT the end of March and during the first days of April when the sap run has ended or is drawing to a close among Northern hills and valleys, a capricious Weather Man often scatters a thin layer of snow over the countryside. It's difficult to predict the coming of the last flurries of the season. After a clear blue-black night when all the sky's candles have been lit and a dawn that brings deep blue overhead with a few scattered rag bags of clouds, gray curtains are drawn suddenly in midforenoon and the sun is shut from view.

Minute by minute the grayness deepens. The mountains across the valley are hidden; the top of the upland pasture behind the farmhouse becomes a dim blotch against the horizon. Then the sugar snow begins. Big, moist flakes wander down through the quiet air. At first the flakes are few and far between. After a short prologue the tempo increases and the act moves swiftly to its climax. The fast-falling snow quickly covers the bare brown patches on the south slopes of the fields, and in a few minutes all the landscape is white.

There's a peculiar quality to the light. A white-grayness rests like a blanket over the land. The roofs of barns, houses, sheds, and corn cribs have a thin clean covering; the R.F.D. box by the roadside has a jaunty beret, and the weathered rocks of the stone walls are a chain-link pattern of white and dark gray. The sap buckets in the sugar orchard catch the snow on their covers, and among the gaunt old maples the saphouse makes a softly etched picture at the height of the storm.

Then, suddenly, the curtain is pulled; gray clouds hurry to the wings, and spring's stage is set again with blue skies, bright sun, and casual white clouds. Sugar snows play a dual role; they are the last reminders of winter and the heralds of the new season.

As the late winter thaws begin to melt the chains of ice, there comes the time of singing waters. On mellow days rivulets run along the sled tracks on the pasture slope where the country-man has been hauling out wood. The trickling waters course around the ends of barns and icehouses, corn cribs and wood-sheds. They flow across the farmyard, into the icy ruts of roads. Listen closely and you can hear their quiet, contented song.

The pasture brook receives tiny streams from the slopes on either side. Often at the edge of spring, snow-melted waters course over the ice that still locks the pebbled brook bed. Meadow brooks overflow their banks, and broad dark bands of water move slowly along toward the river. When cold nights come, the morning sun's jewel gleams are reflected on the thin silvery sheets studded with brown grass stems. On the gentle slopes of mowings, diminutive trickles move slowly among the crowns of the grasses. In the maple-sugar grove, rivulets wind in and out among the massive trunks.

Nature raises her baton in spring, and from countless hills and slopes over the northland the symphony begins as singing waters start their long journey to the rivers and lakes and oceans. The climbing sun sends more direct rays, the south breeze flings out its advance scouts, the season lifts its arm, and the tiny streams begin the soft, slow movement that will soon swell to crescendo. There will be times of hesitation, times when the voice of the first movement will be hushed for a period. But as soon as winter starts its retreat, one knows there will be only delaying actions. When the singing waters begin their tunes, spring is drawing on.

DRUMMING TIME

WHEN the Month of Winds has about run its course, but before mowing fields and upland pastures show the first faint tinge of green, the ruffed grouse chooses a favorite log or hummock and sends his drum call echoing over the countryside. Banks of hard-packed snow still lie in fence corners; snow covers the ground in the shady areas beneath spruces, pines, and hemlocks. Ice formations cling to the brook's banks in the pasture where clear water runs over the gravelly bottom and exposed tree roots.

The grouse feels the thrill of an awakening world when the sun is high and spring is unlocking the land. He is a handsome chap. With his rounded chest, short stubby legs, bright beady eyes, and brown epaulets on his shoulders, he reminds one of the famous Corsican warrior who set out to conquer Europe in the last century. When his temper is up, he spreads his fanlike tail with its decorative band of reddish-brown fringe and lifts his ragged crest.

The drumming act is one of the most interesting sights of the woodland. The drummer usually struts back and forth a few times like a doughty little conqueror. His wings beat against his sides so rapidly the eye cannot follow them. But the staccato noise rolls away through the trees and across the fields. The countryman, spreading dressing on the land, mending fence, or splitting wood, stops his work a moment and listens to the hollow echoing rumble. It's a welcome sound. When drumming time has come again he knows spring is practically here.

SUNSETS can be beautiful in any season, but there is often something especially fine about them during the period when winter is alternately loosening its grip and reasserting its power. Now that one can hear the first faint whispers of the oncoming resurrection, the sunsets of mellowing days paint glorious pictures.

No longer is Earth a helpless prisoner. Snow shrinks away from stone walls and the moss-etched granite chains once more outline fields and pastures. During a sunny day one can almost see the snow disappearing from the countryside. Water trickles down sled tracks and across farmyards. When day's end approaches there is beauty on the land and over the sky. Night's curtain is not so quickly drawn; day and night meet and linger.

When the sun is an hour above the western rim, long horizontal banners color the sky. If moisture conditions are right, there is a vivid painting of reds and yellows, pinks and golds. The low slanting rays pluck shades of purples, violet, chestnut, and steely blues from the granular snow. As the sun drops close, the color in the sky deepens. There is a flaming interlude of scarlet hues; vertical pennants reach high. For a fleeting moment the countryside is starkly illumined in brilliant light. The hardwoods on westerly ridges are slender silhouettes; the trees along the valley river are clearly etched stitching; zigzag rail fences are sharply outlined against the snow.

Slowly the painting in the sky drops closer to the horizon. For a time there is a miniature cameo just above the rim; then deepening shadows climb over the land. Golden lights stream from windows. Darkness deepens and gold stars prick through the deep blue velvet overhead. A late winter sunset marks the end of another day, but its seasonal beauty lifts the heart of him who reads its message.

PICTURE CREDITS

Frontispiece: By Gustav Anderson, from Ewing Galloway, N. Y.

Facing page 1: By Ewing Galloway.

Page 5: By Gustav Anderson, from A. Devaney, Inc., N. Y.

Page 9: By Forsythe, from U.S.D.A.

Page 18: By David W. Corson, from A. Devaney, Inc., N. Y.

Page 25: By David W. Corson, from A. Devaney, Inc., N. Y.

Page 31: By George French.

Page 34: By Gustav Anderson, from A. Devaney, Inc., N. Y.

Page 41: By John H. Vondell.

Page 47: By George French.

Page 50: By Ewing Galloway, N. Y.

Page 57: By Winston Pote.

Page 66: By Philip Gendreau, N. Y.

Page 71: By Caulfield & Shook, from Ewing Galloway.

Page 82: By H. Armstrong Roberts.

Page 89: By Josef Scaylea, from A. Devaney, Inc., N. Y.

Page 96: By A. Devaney, Inc., N. Y.

Page 107: By Ewing Galloway, N. Y.

Page 112: By Gustav Anderson, from Ewing Galloway, N. Y.

Page 117: By George French.

Page 128: By Lee A. Ellis.

Page 137: By G. P. Bond, from Black Star.

Page 144: By Gustav Anderson, from A. Devaney, Inc., N. Y.

Page 149: By E. C. Hunton, from U.S.D.A. Extension Service.

Page 155: By David W. Corson, from A. Devaney, Inc., N. Y.

Page 162: By Gustav Anderson, from A. Devaney, Inc., N. Y.

Page 167: By Gustav Anderson, from Ewing Galloway, N. Y.

Page 178: By David W. Corson, from A. Devaney, Inc., N. Y.

Page 189: By Gustav Anderson, from Ewing Galloway, N. Y.